Figures of

WRITING WITHOUT BORDERS

Writing Without Borders exists to provide space for writing and thought which challenges the norms of academic discourse. Books in the series will touch on Multilingual Matters' key themes – multilingualism, social justice and the benefits of diversity and dialogue – but need not focus entirely on them. Books should be short (20,000–40,000 words is ideal) and represent a departure in some way from what and how you would usually write a journal paper or book manuscript. They may contain experimental writing, new ways of thinking or creating knowledge, topics that are not generally addressed in academic writing, or something we haven't thought of yet…. The series is a place to explore, think, challenge and create. If you are not sure if your idea is 'right' for this series, please ask us.

Writers from the Global South will be particularly welcomed and sought out, as well as writers from marginalised communities and groups within the Global North. Writers from all academic disciplines are welcome, as are experts working in non-academic settings.

Full details of all the books in this series and of all our other publications can be found on http://www.multilingual-matters. com, or by writing to Multilingual Matters, St Nicholas House, 31–34 High Street, Bristol BS1 2AW, UK.

WRITING WITHOUT BORDERS: 2

Figures of Interpretation

Edited by

B.A.S.S. Meier-Lorente-Muth-Duchêne

MULTILINGUAL MATTERS
Bristol • Blue Ridge Summit

DOI https://doi.org/10.21832/DUCHEN9394

Library of Congress Cataloging in Publication Data

A catalog record for this book is available from the Library of Congress.

Names: Meier-Lorente-Muth-Duchêne, B.A.S.S., editor.
Title: Figures of Interpretation/Edited by B.A.S.S. Meier-Lorente-Muth-Duchêne.
Description: Bristol; Blue Ridge Summit: Multilingual Matters, 2021. | Series: Writing
Without Borders: 2 | Includes bibliographical references. | Summary: "This ground-break-
ing book assembles 31 portraits of people who interpret languages, cultures, situations,
institutions and people, and offers graphic interpretations of their collective experience.
They tell a powerful story about the structure of contemporary society and the hierarchical
distributions of power that permeate our lives"-- Provided by publisher.
Identifiers: LCCN 2020043368 (print) | LCCN 2020043369 (ebook) | ISBN 9781788929387
(paperback) | ISBN 9781788929394 (hardback) | ISBN 9781788929400 (pdf) | ISBN
9781788929417 (epub) | ISBN 9781788929424 (kindle edition) Subjects: LCSH: Translating
and interpreting--Social aspects. | Translators--Biography. | Multilingualism--Social aspects.
| Intercultural communication. | Language and culture.
Classification: LCC P306.97.S63 .F54 2021 (print) | LCC P306.97.S63 (ebook) | DDC
418/.020922--dc23
LC record available at https://lccn.loc.gov/2020043368
LC ebook record available at https://lccn.loc.gov/2020043369

British Library Cataloguing in Publication Data
A catalogue entry for this book is available from the British Library.

ISBN-13: 978-1-78892-939-4 (hbk)
ISBN-13: 978-1-78892-938-7 (pbk)

Multilingual Matters
UK: St Nicholas House, 31–34 High Street, Bristol BS1 2AW, UK.
USA: NBN, Blue Ridge Summit, PA, USA.

Website: www.multilingual-matters.com
Twitter: Multi_Ling_Mat
Facebook: https://www.facebook.com/multilingualmatters
Blog: www.channelviewpublications.wordpress.com

The policy of Multilingual Matters/Channel View Publications is to use papers
that are natural, renewable and recyclable products, made from wood grown in
sustainable forests. In the manufacturing process of our books, and to further
support our policy, preference is given to printers that have FSC and PEFC
Chain of Custody certification. The FSC and/or PEFC logos will appear on
those books where full certification has been granted to the printer concerned.

Typeset by in Sabon and Frutiger by R. J. Footring Ltd, Derby, UK
Printed and bound in the UK by the CPI Books Group Ltd.
Printed and bound in the US by NBN.

Contents 1

Random table of contents with names of the figures of interpretation drawn out of a hat by the editors

Contents 2

Random table of contents with names of the figures of interpretation in alphabetical order

Contents 3

Random table of contents with favourite or current laundry detergent of the authors in reverse alphabetical order

Contents 4

DIY

Navigating *Figures of Interpretation*

B.A.S.S. Meier-Lorente-Muth-Duchêne

There was slight indignation on Dr. Marc's face as he described his role as an interpreter at a radio-oncology clinic in the German-speaking part of Switzerland. Dr. Marc was a medical doctor by profession and was employed as such at the clinic. Yet, his biography made him multilingual, having grown up in Luxembourg speaking Luxembourgish and French, and learning German and English as well. As an adult, he also learned Italian, his wife's first language, making him proficient in three of the most widely used languages in Switzerland. This was an important asset for his employers. Dr. Marc, however, did not see the linguistic accommodation of the clinic's patients as falling within his responsibility as a medical professional. He seemed unhappy about how his employer strategically used his language skills, an area of expertise that he believed to be beneath his qualifications.

A group of scholars investigating the role of language in the healthcare marketplace in Switzerland, we were seated around a small table in an office discussing Dr. Marc's experience. We were struck by Dr. Marc's reaction to his language work, how he seemed to perceive it as unbefitting of his qualifications. This feeling stood in stark contrast to those of other people we met at the clinic: secretaries, medical assistants or cleaners. Most of them talked about instances where they had tried to accommodate patients with their linguistic skills, and while these were challenging experiences for some, none of them framed these instances as a waste of their working time. The difference in power, relating to a person's status as well as their economic means, seems to affect how people value their possible involvement in linguistic facilitation and their willingness to do such work. It is this connection that demanded a deeper and more intricate understanding of the practice of interpretation. Dr. Marc stood at the beginning of our journey to collect "figures of interpretation" – portraits of people who interpret. We had set out by investigating the Swiss healthcare market, where we could observe different and differing processes, but the conspicuous omnipresence and invisibility of interpretation surfaced in all our narratives.

Similarities and ruptures unfolded as we discussed and contemplated other people we had met; people who acted as professional interpreters in courtrooms or in the migration regime; others who interpreted as part of their job – as a luggage carrier at an international airport or as a secretary for a multinational company; and yet others who interpreted informally – within a community that organized itself on social media or amongst prison inmates. We felt that their narratives, their practices, their affective responses and material living conditions intricately told us about structures of society, about hierarchical distributions of power permeating everyday life. Interpreters have accompanied expanding empires and colonial conquerors; they have been essential for trade and indispensable for military negotiations amongst potential allies; they have been crucial for missionary work (sometimes being both missionary and interpreter) and have helped maintain, as well as disrupt, the reign of those in power. In contemporary, capitalist society, interpretation has become increasingly standardized and professionalized: there are courses and certificates for people entering paid work in translation and interpretation, as well as additional qualifications for wage laborers in other professions, who may be encouraged or even obliged to go through such training to improve their skills. At the same time, this professionalization is contrasted with the exploitation of the linguistic skills of other wage laborers.

We struggled to find a format that would give space to and produce knowledge about such individual experiences entwined in larger socioeconomic and political processes, to find other ways of writing, distinct from peer-reviewed articles that rely on theory, methodology and the usual claim to authorship of countable publications on which academic careers are built. We felt the need to write in a different form and came up with the idea of short portraits: stories of people and of their practices of interpretation. So we set out in search of such "figures of interpretation," in different geographical, social and professional places and across time. We thought of colleagues and friends who might have something to tell, who have encountered such figures or might know people who could contribute. As the figures arrived, we found that they addressed new issues, indicated different perspectives and served as our orientation for reaching out to other potential authors. And as we received them, we found the collection increasingly multifaceted, fascinating and challenging.

Figures are real people and every real person can be a figure. The understanding of individuals as figures opens a perspective on an individual's life experience that reveals seemingly impersonal conditions of a particular time and place. In this vein, this book assembles historical and contemporary portraits of people who interpret and describes their material living conditions and experiences – a collection that allows us to access and better understand larger structural processes through the singularity of individual trajectories.

And so, we met again in the same office where we started to think about Dr. Marc, piles of paper on the table between us with contributions provided by sociolinguists, social scientists, historians, anthropologists and interpreters. Many shared our interest, had been equally struck by the omnipresence and invisibility of interpretation and the people who provide it. For some, it was only our call for contributions that had made them realize that their informants – themselves or one of their family members – were even engaged in interpretive language work. Many contributors enjoyed the unfamiliar approach to academic knowledge production and were intrigued to write about people they encountered in real life or in archives, whose experiences, they felt, needed to be told and collectively assembled. Some were also puzzled or worried about venturing outside the comfort zone of academic ductus by writing this way.

We were absorbed in thought, our eyes moving between the different portraits we received, trying to see patterns: we discussed a Roman soldier in what would be present-day Slovakia, then turned to a Spanish-speaking person who, 2000 years later, provided *ad hoc* translation between the police and pedestrians entangled in a dispute. The intricate details of the personal lives of people who share only the element of interpreting in their life trajectories, the similar, diverging or even conflicting experiences and narratives, were overwhelming.

Our struggle to find common threads between these figures, to understand what their assemblage uncovered, brought us to an image – the image of a coffee cup tumbling over, a material obstacle that gives way and coffee that spills over the assembled documents, fast at first, then as a trickle, immediately drying in some places, resting in pools in others. As the mess spreads out, a map unfolds, connecting figures of interpretation and their narrators through space and time. The coffee does not spill randomly but follows gravity, textures and ruptures in the paper, over and around objects placed on the table. The map that starts to show the connections between the figures of interpretation is not random either: the paths run along inclinations and tendencies that are shaped by systems of power built on exploitation and domination. The lines show continuities in why people interpret or become interpreters. What seems random from the perspective of the individual is connected to political forces surrounding them. We can see this in the example of Enrique, Magellan's slave, who accompanied him on his conquests, and who suddenly found himself in the role of the interpreter as they sailed into waters unexplored by the conquistadors, where people unexpectedly spoke in words he could understand; Nima, a present-day Iranian immigrant in Belgium, who faced difficulties in finding work in the racist labor market but became a much sought-after interpreter when war made people whose language he understood seek refuge; or Narendra, an Indian who, years after he was urged to acquire Russian skills because of India's past ties with the Soviet Union, was able to access them when Russian-speaking medical tourists started arriving in large numbers in his home country. The map also depicts the physical and emotional dangers that often accompany interpretation and the people providing it. Such was the case of Conrad, a German immigrant during the colonization of what would become the

US, who had to fight for his life against the harsh climate while
hiking for many days to settlements of the Mohawk, whose
language he spoke; Tulay, a young, female interpreter who had
to negotiate her role in a highly patriarchal setting marked by
political conflict on a state visit of a Turkish government delegation to an African country; or Bintou, a court interpreter in
Burkina Faso, who struggled with the emotional toll when she
had to translate the narrative of a child who had been sexually
abused. The lines also reveal continuities and ruptures in the way
interpreters navigate their own roles – as representatives, as mere
transmitters in a communicative event or as actors who can filter
and steer the exchange. This emerges in the stories of Non, a
Japanese interpreter and businesswoman in the Philippines, who
emphasizes the likeness of all human beings but also stresses
the fact that she is perceived as a representative of Japan; Darko
from Serbia, who interprets in medical settings in Switzerland
and struggles with his role within the migration regime, where
he is given little to no agency to take sides with those in danger
of being deported; or Alain, another court interpreter in Burkina
Faso, who values the creativity needed in his profession and
explains how he chooses his words to ease communicative events
that might otherwise result in conflict between the different
parties at court.

As such a map of connections and breaks, faint paths and
moments of intense overlaps and intersections unfolded in our
imagination and discussions, it became clear that the project
could not be restricted to words. It was Nino Paula Bulling
who contributed drawings based on an own reading, an own
interpretation of the assemblage of portraits in this book. The
cover and the 10 drawings inside the book show moments and
feelings that resonate with the experiences of the figures of interpretation, images that can inspire readers to see connections
between them.

Enrique, Nima, Narendra, Conrad, Tulay, Bintou, Non,
Darko and Alain are examples of people who are portrayed in
Figures of Interpretation. Their narratives speak of status and
practices, of different times and places. The collection of their
portraits contributes to an understanding of how language
intersects with race, class, gender and geopolitical space. The

portraits imply various forms of relationship with the "figures" themselves and different ways of writing. Some of the vignettes were written by the figure, some were written in discussion with the figure and others were not read by the figure at all. Some of the portraits are based on encounters from fieldwork or the archive and others are stories about friends or relatives.

They are interpreted individually and, through this book, are open for interpretation collectively and connectively. *Figures of Interpretation*, therefore, also addresses the authors and the readers, who become figures of interpretation themselves. Further, by understanding a figure as a shape or configuration, *Figures of Interpretation* points to the web connecting the people who interpret. Their story is part of a larger history, a history of interpreters, a history of interpretation and a history of interpretive reading. This history can be told because it is built on narratives that are attentive to singular experiences as well as to the underlying hierarchical distribution of power.[1]

Note

(1) We thank the Swiss National Science Foundation for the funding of our research project (no. 159852) which was the starting point of this journey. We thank the Institute of Multilingualism at the University of Fribourg, whose financial support made it possible to have an edited book which not only includes art in words but also art in drawings. We thank Christopher Huguenin for his sensitive work of editing the whole manuscript.

Aïcha

by Aïcha and Maria Rosa Garrido Sardà

Aïcha is a professional journalist who works as a communicator for an international humanitarian agency. She mainly reports publicly on ongoing armed conflicts and explains the agency's mission and operations to civilians and authorities. Her career has concentrated mainly on the Middle East and North Africa (MENA) – with temporary missions in Libya, Yemen and Iraq in the past 10 years – owing to her sought-after Arabic competences, acquired in her home country, coupled with her Francophone education and English competences. Although she uses Arabic in the field and communicates in English and French as institutional languages, her job description does not involve interpreting or translation, tasks reserved for the 'interpreters' in the agency. As a personal goal, this young woman strives to bring visibility to conflicts forgotten by the media, such as the one in Yemen, as well as their victims, *vis-à-vis* the international community, agency donors and news media like the BBC or Reuters. Despite her strong humanitarian vocation to work with and give a voice to those affected by war, the succession of unaccompanied postings in conflict zones with strict security measures has taken its toll on her.

As an Arabic-speaking communicator, Aïcha is close to the war victims and builds trust in the humanitarian agency through face-to-face interactions with local interlocutors, as well as social media. She publicly reports on the agency's activities to a global audience so that it may eventually obtain more funding for humanitarian aid, mainly through campaigns and media appearances. For example, Aïcha spoke to the families of 85 detainees from a prison in northern Iraq who visited their loved ones after years of little or no contact. Her official task was to explain how these families experienced this long separation to a global audience via the agency's website. She communicated with these people in Arabic, even though they spoke different geographical varieties, and made notes of their stories, accompanied by a colleague who took their photographs as they arrived at the prison. Her comprehension of different Arabic varieties owes much to her humanitarian career in the Middle East. But even though she can write in Arabic and French, she wrote this feature story in English, and in-house translators translated it into other working languages, including Arabic.

However, she has also used her mediation skills as an institutional representative who can speak Arabic and English in tasks that are not part of her job description. Expatriate workers are generally expected to be 'flexible', and Arabic speakers in particular are institutionally regarded as (unofficial) figures of interpretation for the humanitarian agency. In Yemen, in the midst of a cholera outbreak in Sana'a's central prison, Aïcha was asked to interpret into Arabic for expatriate co-workers (Italian and Latin American nationals) as an *ad hoc* support, because the agency's interpreters were busy. She was afraid of overstepping her bounds as an *ad hoc* interpreter who should only translate for her colleagues, charged with ascertaining the conditions of imprisonment, rather than engaging in conversation with local interlocutors. Nonetheless, her Arabic family name broke the ice with the prison director. While they chitchatted in Arabic, she had to explain to her colleagues who did not speak Arabic that it was important for her to first establish some common ground and build trust with him in order for them to discuss procedures to contain the outbreak and present the agency's support later on. Aïcha's familiarity with oral culture in the Arabo-Muslim world, including shared stories, gestures and the meanings of the unspoken, greatly facilitate her communication work.

Aïcha has worked for this humanitarian agency for over 10 years. Given the hard and stressful working conditions, she chose to work on fixed-term contracts, in order to be able to take breaks between missions. Working in the field is a very intense experience, with work around the clock, including weekends (especially during crises). Humanitarians working abroad need to join new teams and environments as quickly as possible in volatile field situations. Suffering from post-traumatic stress after a life-threatening situation in the field during her first one-year mission, she was taken out of her second mission in a conflict zone and took a medical break back in her home country. Aïcha decided to take a two-year break, when she worked instead mainly in project management, but she soon needed a different challenge. Despite having requested a short mission, the humanitarian agency offered her an 18-month mission in an ongoing conflict whose intensity forced her to have medical rest in late 2017. As we write in the summer of 2019, Aïcha is on her first mission outside of the Middle East and North Africa. Even though she is no longer 'stuck in the Middle East', as some of her Arabic-speaking colleagues put it, she wants to leave the field because she feels that she has already experienced what the communications department has to offer. Institutionally, she no longer feels in sync with new digital trends in the agency, given her strong preference for contact with victims. She'd like to redirect her career to learning and development in the humanitarian sector, in order to share her know-how and experience.

Geographical mobility has characterized Aïcha's communications career in the humanitarian sector. She also travels for pleasure, because she enjoys photography and discovering new cultures and customs. The two authors, both women from the same generation, met through Maria Rosa's research on the recruitment and management of mobile humanitarians, with a focus on those who speak Arabic. Maria Rosa has become increasingly interested in women's working conditions and experiences in the humanitarian sector thanks to experiences like Aïcha's. They were able to meet in person during Aïcha's debriefing sessions in the agency's headquarters in Maria Rosa's current country of residence. The conversation continues: the two women share life and professional updates with each other.[1]

Note

(1) The views expressed in this contribution are those of the authors and do not necessarily reflect the positioning of the humanitarian agency referred to.

Aijan and Kathleen

by Kathleen Painter

Having made a last-minute decision to take Kyrgyz language classes, I find myself as the only student in a classroom in Bishkek, Kyrgyzstan. At 10am the teacher arrives, turns on the light, and silently writes her name on the board: Айжан (Aijan). She's tall, thin and statuesque. I am struck by her restraint as she introduces the day's vocabulary: first a greeting in Kyrgyz and then a set of familiar terms from Russian for words such as coffee, tea, and markers. It is my first glimpse at how Aijan, through a set of professional practices I don't yet understand, shares interpretations of her country with students as a language teacher in modern Kyrgyzstan.

The director of this private language school, an elderly Kyrgyz woman, founded it shortly after the country's independence from the Soviet Union. There are generally three types of students who come to the school: volunteer workers who are sent by international aid organizations to study Kyrgyz, American undergraduate students who come to study Russian, and Kyrgyzstani students who join the school to study English. Kyrgyz, Russian and the beginner levels of English are taught by Kyrgyzstani teachers, while the upper levels of English are taught by 'native' English-speaking teachers, mostly from the US and UK.

Aijan is one of the longest-serving members of a group of 20 young, female Kyrgyzstani teachers at the school. Their low salaries form a crucial part of the director's business model, enabling her to advertise the school as the cheapest place in the world to study Russian and as one of the only places to study Kyrgyz. Most people within the urban population of Bishkek speak Russian and not Kyrgyz, a result of Soviet Russification policies and the still prevalent idea that Russian is a language of opportunity. And the study of Russian is in high demand in Kyrgyzstan, especially for American students seeking stable government jobs, because it is seen as less political than studying in Russia. However, because of her background, Aijan's Russian isn't considered pure enough to teach at the school. She is one of the only teachers from a mountain community outside of Bishkek, where she lived until her early 20s, when her family chose her a husband and she moved with him to the city. The study of Kyrgyz is less in demand, but Aijan usually has one or two private students in addition to several groups of students for English.

The director controls the Kyrgyzstani teachers with a long list of regulations, high fines for misbehavior, and frequent firings. They are not allowed to sit during classes, discuss personal matters, or wear bright colors. They must smile and provide positive encouragement, but not become friends with students. The time when they are not teaching is spent in a study room with big windows, where they must appear to be working even if they have run out of tasks. The director doesn't bother to learn most of their names, so she requires them to sit in meetings with their name tags facing forward. Most teachers don't last more than six months, and because they must follow the script of the same lesson plans for up to seven classes per day, the work is largely repetitive and requires a lot of patience. Most of them live with their families because they cannot afford rent in the city.

In contrast, Aijan's American and British colleagues at the same school enjoy more professional respect and freedom in their positions. The director has an agreement with a provider of English teaching certificates that guarantees a job upon completion of the course, which helps to ensure a steady flow of these workers. They work four days a week and teach no more than four lessons a day, usually from 2 to 8pm, but their salaries are three times higher than those of their Kyrgyzstani colleagues. They have almost no contact with the director; instead, they are loosely supervised by a British headteacher who has been working at the school since he came to Kyrgyzstan seven years ago. Known for his relaxed attitude and love of the Kyrgyz national football league, he rarely takes on a supervisory or punitive role. The teachers who work with him don't follow any of the same rules as the Kyrgyzstani teachers – they wear what they want, deviate from the curriculum whenever they want, and have been, on occasion, allowed leniency on switching groups or even sleeping through lessons. They live for free in a nearby house or choose to spend part of their salaries on nicer private apartments, and often negotiate multiple months of vacation.

I am one of *these* teachers. Shortly after finishing my master's degree, I found an internship at this school that allowed me to teach English half of the time and to take language classes for the other half. I stopped taking Aijan's Kyrgyz classes after one week, succumbing to the pressure of studying the language that would be more useful – Russian – and decided to apply for a prestigious US-government research grant for nearby Kazakhstan. Whenever I see Aijan in the hallways of the school between classes, she doesn't say anything. She simply sends a double wink – closing both eyes briefly – and this discreet acknowledgment of our time together in class always sends me into reflection about our roles, given the value attributed to the languages we teach and the cultures we are called upon to represent in the process.

While all teaching is interpretive work, this is especially true of language teaching: decisions about what chunks of language and bits of culture to teach and how to teach them are made and mediated by the teacher, who serves, at least temporarily, as an authority on the language and an embodiment of the culture being studied. As such, Aijan's words, behaviors, expectations, explanations, and even professional presence in class are expressions of how she views the world and her place in it. Further, she is called upon in her position to represent a version of Kyrgyz culture that is barely visible in Bishkek, but that is considered – both by locals and foreign aid organizations – to be important for nation-building. There are very few existing teaching materials, so the director has asked Aijan to write much of the Kyrgyz curriculum herself. In class, not only does she show students photos of the mountains near her home and videos of performances of traditional Kyrgyz music, but she also shares vocabulary about domestic violence, hinting at the practice of bride kidnapping and the struggle for gender equality in the country, or vocabulary about exotic birds that are under threat due to a lack of environmental protections. As her students prepare for careers in international development, policymaking, or language education, the ideas she shares will frame their personal interpretations of Kyrgyzstan. Importantly, many of her students will eventually hold positions in the media or government that require them to provide authoritative public interpretations on Kyrgyzstan to English-speaking audiences.

Aijan must also prepare groups of Kyrgyzstani students in lower-level English classes to enter the upper levels with 'native' teachers such as me. As I start to teach, I find it hard to take myself seriously as a representative or authoritative voice on English or American culture. Instead, in the classroom, I see myself as fighting against an idealized view of the US and an inflated idea of the transferrable economic value of English. To cope with these tensions, I work hard to create a relaxed and informal atmosphere. I tell my students when I don't know a British term from the day's lesson and constantly show how there is often more than one acceptable answer to a grammar question. I bring them breakfast on days after tests. When they ask about food from my home state, I make them laugh by showing pictures of fried Oreo cookies from the Texas state fair. Sometimes during our conversations, they tell me about their dreams of becoming programmers in the US and they ask with incredulity if the minimum wage is really so high. I answer as honestly as I can, but then steer the conversation towards what I consider to be the benefits of living in Kyrgyzstan. Over time, I couldn't continue ignoring the fact that almost everyone I met was trying to leave Kyrgyzstan. In fact, work migration is extremely common in the country and almost one-third of the GDP comes from remittances from abroad. So I shouldn't have been surprised when Aijan told me that she had found a better job and planned to go to Dubai to teach.

At the same time, to convince the US State Department that I could act as a 'citizen diplomat' while on my research grant, I had framed my time at the school in terms of Russian language skills, concrete cultural understandings, and awareness of the complexities of conducting research in Central Asia. This allowed me to move to nearby Almaty, Kazakhstan, to continue studying while interpreting the US for Kazakhstani students and Central Asia for an academic audience. Back in Bishkek, Aijan was promoted to a job where she would continue to teach but would also be in the position of having to give out fines to the other teachers – and she decided not to move to Dubai. As I finish writing this vignette, I wonder about the new and ongoing pressures Aijan faces and about what I could have done differently. Even though I discussed the project and this story with Aijan herself in Russian, and shared the vignette in English, I worry that my interpretation of her life and our unequal positions in the school is a blind imposition of my values and is irrelevant or redundant to her. During this process, I spent more time thinking, analyzing, writing, and editing this vignette than being her friend. So if I could go back, I wouldn't do it again.

An Cha

by Mi-Cha Flubacher

Living as a Korean woman in German-speaking Switzerland, married to a Swiss husband and mother to my brother and me, my mother has always been an interpreter, translator and broker of languages, cultures and traditions – of culinary taste, sense of humour, communicative patterns, metalinguistic strategies, even expressions of love. During my childhood visits to Korea, she instructed us on how to behave properly: don't lie down on the floor during meals, even if you're sitting on the floor; bow to your elders; and so forth. In one instance, she had to comfort my brother and me when we were scared of our grandmother, who had appeared to hit us. She explained to us that the vigorous patting of our backs was in fact a sign of affection.

She arrived in Switzerland in the late 1960s as a trained nurse, with a contract at the local university hospital as a surgical nurse. During her teenage years in impoverished post-war South Korea, she had escaped her everyday misery and found comfort in litera- ture, always dreaming of becoming a writer herself. But, for a young woman, there were hardly any options in this direction, especially without financial means. Therefore, going to a nursing school in a local US-missionary hospital, a free training course of three years, was the best option for her. After her training, she was offered work abroad. This path was followed by a whole generation of Korean nurses during the 1960s and 1970s, a para- digmatic example of brain drain from poorer countries to the centre(s) of capitalist production. For example, West Germany maintained bilateral agreements with Korea for female nurses from the mid-1960s until the 1970s. The analogous migration experience for Korean men was working as miners. Trained at an American missionary nursing school in South Korea, my mother did not go to Germany, but first went to Chicago on a work contract. Symptomatically, this contract offered a lower salary than for the locally trained nurses. Even coming from a country ravaged by war and having first-hand experiences of poverty and misery, my mother was deeply troubled by what she witnessed in Chicago, which was an extremely violent city with jarring social inequality. The visible discrimination against the black population was hard to stomach, the culture shock immense, and so she was truly homesick. For some reason, her best friend from nursing school had ended up in Basel, Switzerland, and in her descriptions this place appeared as paradise. This friend arranged everything so that my mother could pack up and move to Switzerland – without knowing a word of German. After settling into her work routine in Switzerland, for which she did not necessarily need German, she decided to change gear. Moving to Fribourg, she enrolled in journalism studies and took a German class. During the semester breaks, she continued to work at the hospital in Basel. For personal reasons, she never graduated, but decided to marry my father, a young trainee doctor she had met there. The two of them soon had my brother and me, with my mother permanently resigning from her career as a nurse.

That my mother did not go crazy home alone with my brother and me is ascribed in our family to the fact that she escaped to the cinema whenever she could. Creating close ties with local cinephiles launching initiatives for alternative spaces to show films, she started to publish film reviews in the Swiss socialist magazine *Vorwärts*. It was these people, my godmother among them, who became curious about the emerging film scene in Korea. When we went to Korea on a family holiday, she was asked to interview Bae Yong-kyun, director of the 1989 breakout hit *Why Has Bodhi-Dharma Left for the East?* for the daily news of the Locarno Film Festival. It was her knowledge of cinema that spoke to this director, who gave her a two-hour interview, which she then translated. Coincidentally, the interview was published one day before Bae received the *Grand Prix* for this very movie at the Locarno Film Festival. It was also she who interpreted for him – Korean to German – at the Q&A after the screening, as well as for his award ceremony.

This mix of interpreting, translating, writing and interviewing soon made up her activities revolving around Korean cinema. It was always her goal to promote Korean cinema internationally. Thus, her actual role was that of a veritable broker for Korean cinema, making use of her linguistic repertoire of Korean, German, French, English and Italian. She translated interviews of varying length from Korean into German and English, was invited by the media to interpret live interviews by journalists (on radio or television, with film journalists, distributors, etc.). She also published articles on films, festivals and filmmakers in German, French, English and Korean. Most importantly, she interpreted for Korean filmmakers, actors, producers and delegations of the Korean film industry in European contexts, as well as for international film people at Korean festivals. In later years (2000–2010), she became a special programmer for the Jeonju International Film Festival, bringing in films from countries, contexts and cultures hardly known by the Korean public (Cuban cinema, censored movies from the Soviet Union, movies from the Maghreb, etc.), with the aim of breaking the hold of mainstream cinema, most powerfully embodied by US film production. Just as she was responsible for the foreign film people in Korea, she was also in charge of Korean delegations in Europe, some of whom were invited on her behalf in the framework of a programme she had launched at various settings and for various occasions throughout Europe.

Even though she never had any training in interpreting and always felt a certain linguistic insecurity in languages other than Korean, she sensed that her professional knowledge of film, and of Korean cinema especially, richly compensated for that. She even witnessed professionally trained interpreters, employed by the embassy and foreign to the cinematic world, struggling with their tasks because they had neither seen the film in question nor knew the director. It was always her strategy to talk to the directors in advance if she had not interviewed them beforehand (which was often the case) or did not know about their career path and artistic development. Even if her interpretation was not linguistically perfect, she knew what the directors wanted to say, and this gave her a lot of confidence. She also often stepped in when directors lost their train of thought in front of thousands of people and volunteered additional information on them, for which they were always very thankful. Usually she and the directors would have agreed on such strategies that depart from the usual interpretation setting. She generally received very positive feedback and she grew close with a few of them over the years. For example, the famous Korean director Im Kwon-taek mentioned to her, after she first interpreted for him at the 1991 Munich Film Festival, that he always took notice of the crowd's reaction in order to get a sense of the quality of the interpretation, which in her case seemed to be very good. She had thus earned his trust and they have remained close friends.

While she did not have negative experiences related to interpretation, my mother's professional trajectory was far from even, oftentimes resembling a roller coaster. Like many other artistic domains, the movie industry in Korea depends heavily on the political economy. This dependence has monetary implications – sparse resources for projects and programmes beyond the lucrative mainstream – but also political ones. Especially under the now ousted president Park Geun-hye, film directors and other artists were systematically blacklisted, disenfranchised or censored. For example, when my mother organized a programme on contemporary Korean cinema in Switzerland in 2015, as part of celebrating the 50 years of diplomatic relations between the two countries, the embassy tried to stop her from showing a politically critical movie by threatening to cut funding. Thanks to moral and financial support within Switzerland, she resisted the official bullying and carried on as planned.

Considering the amount of work she has done, it needs to be said that most of it has been unremunerated. It is telling that she remembers only two instances of remuneration, both outside of the world of cinema: once, she was asked to interpret for the Swiss police, who were interviewing a Korean culprit; another time, she interpreted for a technology company in Switzerland when it hosted a Korean business partner. In the context of cinema, when she was invited to festivals her flights and accommodation were paid for, but she never earned a proper salary for her various activities. While the domain of art production *per se* thrives on self-exploitation, incessantly drawing on all kinds of resources from elsewhere, this critique could be expanded to all forms of unpaid labour, especially that done by women. Thus, in a sense, her work for Korean cinema was only possible thanks to my parents' socioeconomic standing in Swiss society (she was not forced to pursue paid labour as a nurse anymore, but could follow her dreams). Finally, it might have been this economic freedom – from institutional and political ties – that has allowed her to amass the symbolic capital which she finds herself endowed with in Korea. She uses this capital to challenge mainstream and conservative trends, in and beyond cinema, to this day.

Antoine

by Alexandre Duchêne

Next to a luxurious hotel in a busy ski resort in Lapland, I observe a group of middle-aged French tourists visiting an exhibition about the Sami. They are accompanied by a French guide, Antoine. He provides the tourists with a lot of anecdotes, often funny (well, at least some of the tourists laugh), about Sami culture and history, while leading them around the exhibition. Some tourists seem to have little interest. Others drink in his words, attentive to every single sentence that comes out of his mouth. Antoine appears self-assured, knowing his job, without overdoing it. He copes with the heterogeneous interests of his group, anticipating, for those obviously not interested in the exhibition, that the outside park contains animals they have never seen (though in fact these are basically reindeer).

During my fieldwork in Lapland, where we, a group of scholars, are studying the economic and social transformation of the Artic North for several years, I have often seen this kind of tourist group visiting exhibitions, walking in the dark in their black-and-blue or black-and-red snow attire, riding snowmobiles, or feeding domesticated reindeer. I have often admired the patience, the calm, the enthusiasm of their guides who, like Antoine, manage their experience on a daily basis.

Antoine is one of many seasonal workers who are contracted by a foreign travel agent and who act as liaisons for tourists who book their trip through those tour operators. Antoine first came to Lapland 12 years ago from the suburbs of Paris. In his mid-30s, he decided to reorient his professional life (what he did before remains vague) and took a continuing education tourism course in France. He heard about Finland through an alumnus of his school who told him there were job opportunities there.

The job market in France being saturated, the attraction of another place, perfectly unknown and somehow exotic, hence challenging and exciting, made him try his luck in Lapland.

As an experienced agent and guide, Antoine has witnessed the boom in interest of foreign tourists for Lapland, and his job is one outcome. He experiences at first hand the attraction Lapland exercises on foreigner tourists, which has grown steadily over the last years. For him, this increased interest is due to various factors. Antoine believes some traditional destinations have become less attractive due to terrorist attacks (in North Africa for instance). Tourists are looking for safe places, and Finland appears to be very secure. Tourists are also looking for new experiences, and since they have little idea of what to expect in Lapland, it makes this destination exciting and exotic. It is also the attraction of the Artic, the snow, the dark, the clean air, that makes tourists rush to the North to enjoy a climate that might not last forever.

Antoine is one of many workers in the tourism industry of the Arctic North who rush to Lapland during the cold season. Some of these seasonal workers are young adventurers who want to have fun during the winter and are happy to experience the North while earning some money as waiters, ski instructors, guides, or cleaners. This temporary workforce comprises Europeans from all parts of the continent, including Finns from Helsinki or other regions of the country. Some others who are older, like Antoine, are looking for new challenges, seeking a job they would be unlikely to get in their own countries. All these workers are in Lapland because of the need for bodies and infrastructures in order to accommodate the consumers.

Antoine's job is to make sure that everything goes smoothly, to maintain ongoing contact with the tourists during their entire visit. He stays in Lapland from December to the end of March, working every day. He lives in a hotel room in the center of the village, the same place where 'his' tourists stay. He is on duty all the time, dealing with the various problems that can arise. Antoine appreciates his job, even if he always has to cope with the dark and with the fact that he is away from home.

His job relies on the fact that the French tourists are searching for a trip *clé en main*, where all activities will be organized in advance, and where they will not have to worry about where to eat and what to see. Most of them, says Antoine, have very limited English skills, and so they need a French agent who can explain, who can mediate. For Antoine, the French are special; they are bad at foreign languages, in comparison with other groups of tourists who don't need a liaison agent. (Interestingly, I have heard very similar comments from Spanish and Italian guides.) He insists that it is very important for the tourists to know the culture. Through his mediation and interpretation, they can access a world that is, in his view, very different. Over the years, Antoine has learned some words of Finnish, not to communicate with the locals, with whom he uses English, but to be used in the activities where he informs the tourists about cultural aspects of the region.

Antoine's job relies on the basic assumption that a particular set of customers has to be served in their language in order for them to get full access to the experience of the North. The knowledge of the place that he has acquired over the years allows him to identify interesting spots and to share with the tourists, in French, his own understanding of the place. His job also relies heavily on the growing interest of this particular set of tourists in the North. The airport is expanding massively, allowing it to accommodate up to 12 airplanes at once. The hotel business is booming. Demand is high. This makes Antoine believe his job is safe.

I'm not completely sure I share his optimism, due to what I have seen here and elsewhere. I recall that Antoine has no permanent contract and he is never sure that he will be hired for another season. I cannot ignore the fact that the tourism business is constantly in search of diversification. A tour operator might gradually target new market segments (a popular sport in the industry), younger tourists for instance, who might be less interested in the activities Antoine proposes, and who might also not be that interested in being accommodated in French, because they don't need it and would rather look for international, transnational companionship. Furthermore, the attraction of the North might also become saturated at some point, given the fickle nature of consumerist practice. In the region, concerns about climate change also impact the lives of locals and foreign workers. The season is less previsible than it used to be and the industry is dealing with situations where the snow is delayed, which impacts massively on the satisfaction of visitors. What Antoine does here thus heavily depends on who is consuming what, how the who and what should be managed. This is exactly what is unstable and not that easy to anticipate. And, presumably, what makes Antoine's interpretative job precarious.

This piece was written before the Covid-19 pandemic.

Arnaldo

by Arnaldo Bernabe Jr

Everything has happened so fast that my mind is on autopilot. The cop car lights flash in my eyes as I stand between a London Metropolitan Police officer and a Spanish-speaking couple, Hector and Xiomara, who ask for my help relaying to the police that they have just been assaulted. The police officer stares at me blankly and asks me to explain what the couple are saying in Spanish. "Hector said he was walking with his girlfriend Xiomara on the way to the metro when the gentleman over there with the dog got in front of him and began saying 'You don't belong here,' and, 'Who do you think you are?'" I say to the officer. The officer seems unaffected, and I return my gaze to Hector, who continues in Spanish, "Y despues empezó a insultar mi novia diciendole puta y cuando hemos intentado de irnos empezó a gestar como si iba a soltar el perro" ("Afterwards, he began to insult my girlfriend, calling her a bitch [prostitute], and when we tried to leave, he began threatening to release the dog"). Tears run down Hector's face on this last part. "Wait right here," the officer says, as he walks over to the gentleman with the dog whom Hector had been referring to.

Incidentally, for the past five months, I have encountered similar situations in the fieldwork and research for my master's dissertation. When I moved to London only three years ago, I unknowingly moved into London's largest Latinx community. As a Latinx New Yorker of mixed-race Puerto Rican descent, some of the small Latinx businesses in South London vaguely reminded me of the Latinx Caribbean community I had left behind in the Bronx. Moreover, some of the closest friends I have made in South London are Spanish-speaking Latinxs, mostly Bolivians and Colombians. These friendships, welded through conversations in Spanish, provided me with a sense of familiarity related to my own Puerto Rican/Latinx identity, as well as some insight into the Spanish-speaking Latinx London experience. In addition, word soon spread that I was an English teacher who worked at a college in London, "y tambien es Latino" ("and he is Latin too"). At times, friends or neighbors would request assistance translating a document, calling a mobile phone company on their behalf, translating at a police station in a domestic violence case or explaining a work contract written in English. Simultaneously, I was contemplating a research topic for my master's degree dissertation. I spent hours in the library brainstorming ideas until a mental breakthrough occurred after attending a talk by Cathy McIlwaine. The Queen Mary University professor had shared her research on the invisibility of the Latinx community in London. McIlwaine's work was the first time I had seen my friends and my London neighborhood contextualized in research. Reading her work gave me license to view my friends' experiences as worthy of research. Thus, I created the project "La lucha continua: How language affects the socioeconomic mobility of Latinx Londoners". The Spanish portion of my dissertation title was borrowed from graffiti scrawled across several London universities (SOAS, UCL and Birbeck) in 2016. At the time, I was completing my master's degree at UCL and Latinx university cleaners were simultaneously organizing due to their precarious working conditions.

Therefore, on that Saturday morning, when I found myself awoken from my slumber by a woman screaming in Spanish, "Por favor! No! El perro!" ("Please! No! The dog!"), I immediately felt responsible to offer help translating to the police because my previous experience with other Latinx Londoners seeking police counsel was that language seemed to pose a barrier to practicing self-agency. Through my sleepy haze I walked to my window and saw the tussle between Hector and the dog-owner. As I watched the two men grapple and punch at each other, sirens cut through the air and two London police cars appeared. Without further hesitation, I exited my apartment and entered the scene myself.

The air is tense and awkward as the three of us wait for the officer to return. "De donde sois?" ("Where are you from?"), I ask the couple as we wait. "Yo de Venezuela y ella de Ecuador"

("I'm from Venezuela and she's from Ecuador"), he responds. Without provocation, the two of them begin to weep as they recount bits and pieces of their story. My eyes shift down to Hector's shirt and, as if on cue, he says "Aqui me mordio el perro" ("Here is where the dog bit me"). His lower back and one of his thighs are slightly punctured, and blood trickles down his brown skin. I look back up at his face. His lip is busted and his cheek is swollen. I turn my gaze over to where the dog-owner is standing, a pitbull at his side. He seems nonchalant, nodding his head as the officer speaks to him in low tones. I look in front of us, where another officer is listening as two neighbors explain what they witnessed. "I was sat in front of my house. I saw the whole thing happen," says one neighbor. "I saw it too," the second neighbor confirms. According to both, the couple turned the corner when the gentleman with the dog crossed the street and blocked their path. He began threatening the couple with his dog and shouting, "Go back to your country!" As I listen to this, a sense of relief and hope burgeons. I have already cast the dog-owner in my mind as the antagonist based on the neighbors' eyewitness accounts. Thus, I'm assuming the police will see the couple as I am imagining them: victims of racially charged violence. My own idea of justice will be served. The dog-owner will be arrested. The evidence is convincing.

My ruminating is interrupted and my body tenses up as I observe the officer returning. "Okay, so he denies starting the fight, and, since I cannot prove who started it, both of you will have to be arrested and taken into custody for at least 24 hours," the officer explains. I translate the message to the couple: "El dice que…" and I am flabbergasted as my words mask my true thoughts: *Officer, why haven't you spoken to your colleague and the two neighbors who witnessed the commotion and have confirmed the dog-owner was the aggressor?* But no, I neatly pack and mentally compartmentalize my ideas into submission. Who am I to assume what this couple wants me to say, right? Instead, I translate the officer's message into Spanish, and Xiomara bursts into tears as Hector watches her and then directly stares into my eyes. "There is a second option," the officer says, interrupting the couple's emotional reaction. "Hay otra opcion" ("There's a second option"), I say. "So we have this law…" – Did he say law or did he say something else? I can no longer recall. My shock in the moment has clouded my ability to clearly remember his words verbatim. "So we have this ... which means that, since I cannot determine who began the fight, if you agree to not press charges and walk away, then I won't arrest you and you would be free to go. But you have to agree to walk away right now and not start any trouble once I leave," the officer explains. As I translate his message, the crying couple respond with nods. "Si ok, solo queremos continuar en camino a la estacion que mañana curro y necesito recargar mi tarjeta de metro." ("Okay, we just want to continue on our way to the train station to refill my transport card because tomorrow I have to work"), Hector says. "Right, okay. I will notify the other gentleman that you've agreed to walk away from this and not press charges," the officer says and walks in the direction of the gentleman with the dog. I look over and the dog-owner nonchalantly stands there, his dog gently wagging its tail. There are no tears running down his face. He lowers his eyes and nods as the officer, again in lowered tones, speaks to him. *What is going on right now? Are you seriously not going to say anything?* My thoughts are urging my mouth to speak. However, I do not want to mistakenly assume I know what is best and speak on the couple's behalf. What if they are undocumented, such as was the case with one of my research participants? Speaking up may lead to the officer asking them for identification. Thus, my attempt to be a neutral translator is correct, right? The truth is that I am unsure, insecure and at complete odds with myself, so I remain silent. The officer returns. "Okay, let them know they are free to go," the officer concludes. I tell the couple, in Spanish, they can leave. "Muchas gracias" ("Thank you"), they say, and walk away. The police officers return to their car, the engine starts, and they pull away. The other man and his dog walk off towards the park. The scene has finished. Everyone is free to go, and yet my mind is trapped in the situation.

I silently return home questioning if I should have spoken up. I further question myself on what my decision-making during translating accomplished on the couple's behalf. The question is mentally burdensome, and, unsure of how to overcome the feeling, I resign myself to the thought that my translating perhaps played a part in reproducing the social hierarchy. "Agree to disagree and keep moving along," as the officer less eloquently phrased it to Hector and Xiomara. And in similar fashion, but not by choice, I accept that I must agree to disagree with myself and move on.

Arokiam and the Unnamed Catechist

by Shanthini Pillai

Catechists played an important role in colonial missionary outposts as lay auxiliaries to European clergy, often assisting in sacramental events such as baptisms and funerals, as well as conveying religious instruction to local Catholic communities. The latter often involved orally interpreting and communicating the tenets of the Catholic faith to prospective or recent converts in their native tongues. I encountered two Tamil lay interpreters of religious instruction in the pages of a memoir written by a French missionary, René-Marie-Michel Fée of the Société des Missions étrangères de Paris (MEP), operating in one of the northern states of colonial Malaya in the late 19th century. One catechist is named Arokiam, while the other unnamed. The anonymity of the latter may have a lot to do with the fact that his catechetical efforts are not wholly recognised by his French superior, and he thus remains on the margins.

When Fée wrote his memoir, Arokiam had spent 30 years of his life as a catechist in Catholic churches catering to the Tamil community in the northern Malay states of Penang and Perak. Described as having a brazen brow and an imposing moustache, Arokiam was quite the household name among the Penang clergy, having earned the nickname Saint Anthony early on in his career, when he was a catechist in one of the parishes on the island of Penang. He owed this moniker to the following incident.

One night, as Arokiam lay sleeping in his quarters at the parish church he was assisting at, he had dreamt that Saint Anthony had appeared before him and conveyed the urgency of attending to a number of reforms in the parish. Arokiam, extremely thrilled at what he saw as a divine selection to be a messenger, immediately sought the presence of his superior, the French priest, Father Hab, of the MEP. Hab, however, was not inclined to believe Arokiam and, instead, proceeded to admonish the Tamil catechist by claiming that, since Saint Anthony was not the patron saint of the parish, which was dedicated to Saint Francis Xavier, its administration was not any of his concern. He then added that, if at all a saint should deign to descend to the parish with a message, the rightful recipient would be the presiding priest and certainly not his assistant. Stonewalled by the hegemony of the Catholic institutional hierarchy, Arokiam was forced to descend into silence, never again to speak of this or any other similar visions that he may have had in the course of his time as a catechist in Hab's parish.

However, brazenness was not only stamped on Arokiam's physical features. He was not content to sit in silence for long. In the 30 years that he carried out his duty as lay catechist for Tamil Catholics among the various churches in Penang, he was dismissed at least 10 times when he fell out of favour with his superiors, the French MEP priests. Arokiam obviously interpreted his role as a catechist as being more than a mere assistant to the French priests. Even during the times when he was not formally appointed in a particular church, he worked fervently to spread the Word in Tamil among the Indian community in Penang. As such, the Penang clergy always ultimately accepted him back into the fold for as much as he disrupted the reign of ecclesial power, his acts of voluntary catechesis ultimately mended the very tears he had made in the fabric. This was probably tied to the fact that he was contributing to the main objective of the missionaries, which was evangelism for the increasing number of converts. French missionaries in Pondicherry had already begun translating Latin and French Roman Catholic bibles, catechisms and other instructional material into Tamil, continuing earlier efforts by the Portuguese. These texts were subsequently used by the MEP missionaries as they travelled to various eastern outposts with Tamil communities, such as the one in Malaya. These missionaries were required to study the languages of the communities that they were to evangelise among. In the case of Malaya, it would have been Tamil and Mandarin, as well as Malay, the native language of Malaya. Yet, they often relied on their lay catechists to reach out to the respective communities. The majority of the Tamil community that the missionaries catered to were of the working class, located in surrounding plantations, as well as the ports, road and railway sites. Most were literate in the Tamil language. Arokiam's familiarity with Tamil and its everyday nuances would have played a significant role in garnering flocks for the missionaries. He would have used the Tamil catechism texts in the same manner as the second, unnamed catechist that I encountered in the memoir.

The unnamed catechist was rather interesting, as he had started out as an unwilling aid to his mother's conversion to Catholicism, though he himself had not converted at that time. We are told that, initially, this man was rather hostile towards his mother's intention to leave the Hindu fold. However, as his mother was unable to read or write, she needed her son's help in relaying the content of the Tamil catechism texts to enable her to learn the religion. Filial piety led him to agree to his mother's requests, and he began to read pages from the Tamil catechism text to her every day. As the unnamed catechist engaged with the various prayers, litanies, Lives of the Saints, as well as various other doctrine contained in the texts and conveyed them orally, in Tamil, to his mother, he was inevitably drawn deep into the tenets of the Catholic faith. In his role as a cultural mediator of the Roman Catholic Tamil texts, the contents that he elucidated daily imbued not only the consciousness of his mother as the prospective convert, but his own too. Months later, after his mother had converted to Catholicism, he approached the French missionary and asked to be baptised as well. The missionary proceeded to put his knowledge to the test and, after a few sessions, found that the young man was indeed quite familiar with the religion and gladly proceeded with his baptism into the faith. Thus, the interpreter is himself transformed by the very act of interpretation. Crossing the boundaries from outsider to insider, the unnamed catechist progressed from a reluctant collaborator in his mother's conversion to a learned participant who willingly embraced the Catholic faith. Yet, the young man was not content with mere conversion. Having experienced the role of informal catechist to his mother, he sought out the missionary again, to formalise this with a catechist diploma. Unfortunately, the missionary denied his request and bade him to return to his employment as a cook. Refusing to take notice, the self-appointed catechist proceeded to carve his own evangelical path, which, unfortunately, led him astray into the darker depths of religious zealotry, when, one day, armed with a knife, he attacked a local Muslim procession. His exegesis of the religious texts from the first point of contact were consequently undone by this incident, and he was never heard from again.

The stories of these two Tamil men in colonial Malaya and the dialogics of their encounter with the Catholic faith are significant to me on a number of levels. Their presence in the French missionary's memoir offers insights into accounts of Tamil lay interpreters of the Catholic faith that often remain unheard. As their stories are threaded into the missionary's main narrative, the significance of their role becomes evident. It was their everyday interpretations and elucidations of the Catholic faith in the Tamil vernacular, alongside the missionaries, that led local congregations to grow. Equally important were their own wilful acts of lay interpretation of messages from sacred figures of saints and catechism texts. These ultimately reveal their own interpretation of their place in the larger evangelical mission, often transgressing boundaries set by their French superiors. They also lead me to deliberate on other such palimpsests that lie hidden within the pages of missionary reports, and what narratives may unfold through my own critical interpretation as I proceed further in my research on the Tamil catechists of Malaya.

Bernardino

by Bernardino Tavares

As a fresh PhD holder and Cape Verdean migrant, I have just entered the interpreting business in Luxembourg. This is the result of my networking efforts to find a job after finishing my PhD studies. Thus, on a friend's referral, I got the opportunity to start off as a freelance 'intercultural mediator', someone who should be competent enough in at least one of the three official languages of the country used by teachers and other school agents, French, German and Luxembourgish, as well as in a language used by migrant parents, who in most of the cases share the same country of origin with the respective mediator. The mediator is employed by the Ministry of Education to facilitate communication between the teachers and those parents. The language industry has been central in Luxembourg's economy and polity as a multilingual country.

I came to Luxembourg after living and studying in Portugal and France. I initially came alone but, after five months, my family – my wife, our little son and daughter – joined me. From April 2014 to April 2017, I worked as a doctoral researcher at the University of Luxembourg, on a project on migration from two Lusophone African countries: Cape Verde and Guinea-Bissau. Then, I had a one-year extension contract to finish writing my thesis, which critically focused on Cape Verdean migration and the role of language and 'loopholes' in Luxembourg's labor market. Now, I am portrayed (by the media, but also by Cape Verdean migrants) as the first Cape Verdean holding a PhD in Luxembourg. I am proud of my trajectory, but sad at the same time for being portrayed like this, despite the long history of Cape Verdean migration to Luxembourg (since the 1960s). This has made me visible, or, rather, over-visible. I am aware that, globally in Europe, there are increasing challenges for fresh PhD holders in finding jobs. Beyond my professional qualifications, social qualities and language repertoire, I also interpret my current job condition in Luxembourg as largely impacted by the combination of my societal positioning as a Cape Vardean migrant and as a PhD holder. Due to the sheer number of requests for interpreting services with Portuguese-speaking parents which the Ministry of Education received from primary and secondary school teachers, I started as a freelance mediator without any prior specific training, which I had a chance to take some weeks later. My task consists in providing interpreting services, using French, Portuguese and Cape Verdean Creole. So far, I have interpreted for parents originally from Portugal, Cape Verde, Angola, Guinea-Bissau and Brazil. Basically, I am a facilitator of communication between Lusophone parents and Luxembourgish teachers during the evaluation periods – or *Bilan* periods – at the end of every trimester, when teachers at public primary and secondary schools inform parents about their children's grades. I have also assisted psychologists testing pre-school pupils' language development at *Centres de Logopédies*.

Interpreting is something I did not plan for. I embarked on it as a way to open gates to employment. I took it up as a temporary occupation to help my financial condition, support my family and broaden my network. Interestingly, I am gaining lived experience and knowledge of praxes and pitfalls in the education system that have stigmatized some pupils of Lusophone background. Such problems are often referred to in newspapers articles, reports and societal discourses addressing the highly unfair German-only literacy system in most public schools in Luxembourg. However, it has been a very unpredictable line of work for me; today I may have too much to do, but tomorrow or after tomorrow I may have nothing. Furthermore, in some encounters, the teachers and parents are strangers to both me, the mediator, and to each other. For the first encounter, excepting names, phone numbers and the pupil's grade, the mediator usually does not have any prior information about the situation or about possible previous teacher–parent interactions.

Although my education trajectory is intrinsically linked to interpretation, since it concerns the study of languages and migration, I hesitated a bit in the beginning due to my insecurity concerning the French language. However, I have managed well so far and, sometimes, when I lack a more precise word in French, I resort to English, in which I have greater competence. I am also mindful of the usefulness of body language to facilitate the communicative event while translating. Likewise, some teachers resort to other communicative resources (gestures, visual aids, pointing to or showing objects etc.) when they cannot find a French word. For the most part, it has been an interesting collaborative experience.

One can often pick up on tensions between the teachers and parents from the very beginning of the encounter. Some teachers are very mechanical and say things abruptly, in a way that might shock the parents. In one case, the teacher just projected the *Bilan* in French onto the board and asked me to translate it directly into Portuguese. It was the most negative *Bilan* I have ever seen, without a single positive comment. The mother did not ask any questions, even when I advised her to do so. It occurred to me that this might be a very serious problem. This was confirmed when, a few minutes later, I found the mother, very nervous, crying in the corridor downstairs on her way out of the school. It is not easy for a mediator to be the bearer of such bad news to parents concerning the educational performance of their children. In addition, I sometimes saw striking contradictions between teachers of German and teachers of French in their narratives about their Lusophone pupils' school performance. The first often use phrases like, "s/he is too slow," "s/he does not ask," while the second often say, "s/he is very motivated," "s/he works well, and if s/he does a little more on this or that, s/he will be fine." I should stress that most of the teachers are usually cordial and respectful, both towards the parents and towards me as the mediator.

My role as an intercultural mediator is constrained by the principle of impersonality. It does not leave me much room to express my views, even when interactions go contrary to what I believe as a Lusophone migrant, as a father and as a researcher. My participation as an intercultural mediator has even reinforced my negative views about the system. My freedom of speech during these encounters is limited to passing the message from one side to another, but I have to ask questions when I do not understand the message. What I observe during professional encounters may not be disclosed to the higher authorities, except when explicit grave tensions and emotional moments occur. Some teachers have even highlighted this hierarchized upward communication pathway to me. To a certain extent, this is a form of control that helps to maintain the status quo, freezing chances for positive change through secrecy and limiting the mediator's ability to speak out during these often emotional encounters. It also contributes to masking public contestations of the system.

I am in between and should not take sides. There are moments when I feel as if I am there as a third party, not as a mediator only, but rather as a silent witness. Sometimes, there is no need to translate, because the parents can get by very well in French. But, on other occasions, I feel as if I am rendered invisible by historical conditions. For example, while it is not mentioned explicitly, I have observed that some Portuguese parents do not feel comfortable with my presence. The mere presence of a mediator affects the communication in important ways. The mediator can have access to very personal information regarding, for example, the parents and their family in general. Moreover, being a mediator originally from a former colonized country translating to parents originally from its former colonizer country may affect the interaction in peculiar ways. For example, when I presented myself as the mediator ("translator" is often used instead of "mediator") in one case, the mother stated, in an uneasy way, "Não, não, eu comprendo tudo, não há problema" ("No, no, I can understand everything, there is no problem"), even though this was not the case. In other cases, while waiting in corridors for the teacher who asked for my services, I have been addressed as one of the parents by teachers and other school staff wondering what I need. Thus, it is extremely important to me to clearly present myself as a mediator beyond the reception and along some school corridors to avoid misassumptions at first glance.

I do not want to be a mediator who helps to maintain the "reign of power" through an unequal educational system. Rather, the social and historical conditions informing my identity as a Lusophone African migrant in Luxembourg mostly urge me to act in order to disrupt this "reign of privilege" in the society I'm now part of. I am still struggling to find ways to deal with this very unequal system, in which most teachers are central figures who maintain it through elaborate discursive conduct. However, at least I feel like I'm finding such ways by sharing my experience here. This is a dilemma for me, due to my limited freedom to express my views during the interactions, even as this job allows me to fulfill my responsibilities despite the precariousness of life after my PhD. I want to be a mediator fully acting for positive social change! Maybe I am a dreamer! But I hope I am not the only one!

Bintou and Alain

by Natalie Tarr

Bintou was actually not very interested in working as an inter-preter at the penal court in Ouagadougou. On the contrary, the idea of sitting in a courtroom all day long, translating one case after another did not figure very high on her list of priorities workwise. And days can run on for very long at penal courts in Burkina Faso, forcing court personnel to stay put for up to eight hours with no or only very short breaks. In 1998, Bintou was in her last year of secondary school, about to sit the final school qualification exams, the *baccalauréat* or bac exams. She had a baby to take care of and she was pregnant with her second child. All she wanted was to successfully finish her high school studies, have her baby and start looking for a decent job. 'Decent' meaning a job corresponding to her qualifications: Bintou already had a diploma in accounting and very soon she was going to pass the bac exams. In fact, accounting was what she loved doing and was good at. Consequently, the interpreting job at the court did not qualify as decent, in her view. The pay was miserable and the hiring criteria ridiculous, Bintou told me: all the Ministry of Justice asked a court interpreter to bring to the job was a primary school diploma. Why suffer through the bac exams if, in the end, she took a job that required qualifica-tions well below hers?

But her older brother insisted. He was the head of the depart-ment of administration and finances at the Ministry of Justice and told Bintou that the penal court was desperately looking for interpreters. Burkina Faso had ratified the UN Covenant on Civil and Political Rights, which states that all defendants in penal cases have the right to be tried in a language of their choice if they do not understand the language of the court. The language used in Burkinabe courts is French, the former colonial language, which today is the so-called official language of the country. When I ask, no judge, prosecutor or lawyer can tell me, however, what the designation 'official language' means in everyday terms, even though government officials seem to agree that this indicates that French needs to be spoken in all government spaces. Since Ouagadougou is the capital of Burkina Faso, it was imperative the penal court there found and hired an interpreter as quickly as possible – as an example for the rest of the country, Bintou told me. When we met in late 2019, I was in Burkina Faso conducting research on the role of translation and of interpreters working at penal courts. Luckily, Bintou was at leisure to talk to me about her experiences working as a court interpreter back in the early 2000s. Now, she was about to start working at the commercial court in Ouagadougou, her interpreting days a long time in the past.

Working for the Ministry – for any ministry, for that matter – means being hired as a public servant, a *fonctionnaire*, and being employed as a *fonctionnaire* conveys upon a person not only a certain status society regards as worthy of respect, but also comes with a reliably paid salary, even if this salary is ridiculously small. In Burkina Faso, many high school students dream of the security a job as a *fonctionnaire* represents. So, in the end, Bintou took the job as a court interpreter, in spite of her reservations, and started translating at the penal court in Ouagadougou in February 1998. Once one is hired as a government employee or public servant, there are opportunities to advance and rise within the system after a certain number of years of service, she knew. And this is what Bintou did.

During her work as a court interpreter, Bintou had to learn to be tough. Not only were the days long, the salary ridiculous, and recognition and respect from other employees of the court near zero, the toughest thing of all was that you had to translate cases that were hard to bear. Once, Bintou had to translate in a rape case. The victim was a four-year-old girl. "You are a human being, a mother, so I could not just turn off my feelings … listening to this small girl and having to translate her words was almost unbearable for me," she told me. Indeed, I had learned that merely observing penal trials for months on end did not make certain facts any more tolerable, but at least I, the Swiss researcher, did not have to repeat and translate what victims and defendants said. "I was crying, tears streaming down my cheeks. All the while I continued to translate the little girl's words for the judge just as my job demanded I do," Bintou continued.

Today, Bintou is not working as court interpreter anymore, having taken advantage of the system that allows *fonctionnaires* to climb the career ladder from the inside. Her children are both at university, studying medicine. Bintou is now head of court scribes at the commercial court in Ouagadougou – and never misses interpreting one second.

Similarly, in Bobo-Dioulasso, another court interpreter was hired to translate penal trials. Alain, just like Bintou in Ouaga-dougou, has long working days, interpreting for many hours at a time. When he is not interpreting, Alain does different clerical tasks around the courthouse. But in one thing, he is luckier than his colleagues in Ouagadougou: due to his love of regular snacks, Judge Patousongo integrates several short breaks into the working day. Court interpreter Alain has to wait outside, however, not being invited to join the judges in culinary camaraderie. During one of these breaks, he starts telling me about his work.

Like Bintou, Alain became a court interpreter somewhat unintentionally. He had volunteered at the penal court as a secretary, following a government campaign which offered unemployed young people administrative jobs, integrating them into the job market. A friend of his working at one of the courts in Bobo-Dioulasso had arranged for him to try out for the job of court interpreter. Alain spoke both Jula, an international language spoken in large parts of West Africa and the main language used in Bobo-Dioulasso, and Moore, one of the larger of 70 languages spoken in Burkina Faso. In addition, having attended some years of high school, Alain also spoke and un-derstood French well enough for this kind of work. These were the hiring criteria he had to fulfill for this job – to be fluent in French and at least Jula. Of course, most judges and prosecu-tors in both Ouagadougou and Bobo-Dioulasso speak the local idiom – Moore in Ouagadougou, Jula in Bobo-Dioulasso – but since government officials insist that the official language be spoken in court, this is what they do. But hardly any Burkinabe use French as a family language or consider themselves to be 'confirmed Francophones'. This designation is used to describe those sufficiently fluent in French to be able to conduct everyday dealings in the former colonial idiom. In Bobo-Dioulasso, Jula is the language of everyday encounters, however, and only those people who have had at least some years of schooling speak sufficient French to fall into the category of 'confirmed Francophone'. 'We translate for our compatriots', as Bintou had described the work she and all court interpreters did.

So, Alain fulfilled the hiring criteria the penal court in Bobo asked of a court interpreter – he spoke Jula, Moore and French. But, unlike Bintou, he had no diploma beyond a middle school certificate, so getting a job interpreting at the penal court was a good opportunity for him to get a foot in, even if this job is often riddled with incomprehensible or dangerous situations, as he describes the work. But let us listen to Alain tell the story himself:

Lors d'une audience correctionnelle en 2015, nous avons assisté, impuissants à un drame, un vieux qui avait commis un acte grave. Il était à la barre et le juge devait prononcer la sentence, mais avant il m'a dit en langue mooré de répéter au juge de ne pas le condamner à une lourde peine sinon il allait le regretter, et je n'ai pas voulu transmettre les dires du vieux. Malheureusement, le juge comprenait parfaitement le mooré et m'a sommé de traduire fidèlement ce que le vieux a dit, alors j'ai hésité et ensuite j'ai prié au fond de moi et dit ce qu'il voulait entendre. Alors tout le tribunal était pris de peur, mais le juge en question n'a pas hésité une minute de plus et a collé huit ans ferme au vieux. Nous sommes à l'audience jusqu'à la descente. Quand nous sommes rentrés, chacun chez soi, plus tard nous apprenons que le juge qui avait prononcé les huit ans ferme contre le vieux là est devant la porte de sa cour et qu'il était à moitié paralysé. Coïncidence ou réalité africaine? Que Dieu nous garde! Cela m'a beaucoup choqué dans mon métier d'interprète judiciaire. Vraiment.

During a penal trial in 2015, we witnessed a drama, powerless, of an old man who had committed a heinous deed. He was in the dock and the judge was about to announce the verdict, but before he could do so, the old man told me in Moore to tell the judge not to condemn him to any harsh punishment, or else he would regret it. Unfortunately, the judge understood Moore perfectly and ordered me to faithfully translate what the old man had said. So, I hesitated, prayed silently to myself, and then I translated what the judge wanted to hear. The court was gripped with fear, but the presiding judge did not hesitate one minute longer and condemned the old man to eight years in prison. We continued holding trials until the end of the day. When we had all returned home, we heard that the judge who had given the old man eight years of prison was outside the door to his compound and had gone half lame. Coincidence or African reality? May God protect us! This has shocked me a lot in my work as a court interpreter. Really.

So, the *métier* of court interpreter does bear certain risks. The person translating can be a victim to headaches, or used by defendants as a mediator with judges, like Alain was in the case he described. Court interpreters also suffer with the victims, having emotional breakdowns, crying, like Bintou in the instance of interpretation she told me about. Bintou is happy not to have to translate such stories anymore. For Alain, these instances are part of what makes court interpreting intriguing, maybe even dangerous. If only the pay were better, he repeatedly mentions, agreeing with Bintou, because then he could more easily care for his growing family.

Conrad

by Aneta Pavlenko

British colonies in North America are not the first place we think of when it comes to the history of interpreting, yet it is worth recalling that in colonial New York and Pennsylvania Indians won the first round of culture wars. Their tongues were accommodated by interpreters, treaties followed Indian protocol and the high costs of hosting large Indian delegations were borne by colonial authorities. In 1763, Sir William Johnson, British Superintendent of Indian Affairs in the northern colonies, complained to the Lords of Trade of severe shortages in qualified personnel:

> Good Interpreters are very necessary here, and are hard to be found, for although I am often thro' their ignorance obliged to deliver my own speeches and generally to explain them, yet the Indians always expect to be treated with an Interpreter. (Letter to the Lords of Trade, November 13, 1763, in O'Callaghan, 1856: 579)

To negotiate land treaties, convey secret messages and schmooze with trusted informants, colonial authorities needed people with insider knowledge of Indian protocol (who speaks first, when to hand out gifts, what to do with the wampum belt) and the metaphors and allegories that permeated Indian oratory. Iroquois experts, for instance, had to know that the terms 'strong and big Rock' and 'Big Mountain' referred, respectively, to Oneidas and Onondagas, not any features of the local landscape. Superintendent Johnson, who learned Mohawk and had a Mohawk common-law wife, Molly Brant, knew first-hand how elusive such mastery was:

> It is only to be acquired by a long residence among them, a daily intercourse with them, and a desire of information in these

> matters Superseding all other considerations. (Letter to the Earl
> of Hillsborough, August 21, 1769, in O'Callaghan, 1849: 947)

Not surprisingly, few individuals had the requisite skills, and
even fewer inspired trust. Natives who picked up English had
little understanding of British customs. Christian Indians,
educated in colonial schools, often forgot their own tongue
(and if not, were mistrusted by their heathen brethren) and the
loyalties of 'half-breeds' and Europeans who went native were
automatically suspect to the English. Fur traders were despised
by both sides: Indians saw them as rascally fellows who added
stones to scales to swindle them of deerskins, while officials
viewed them as ignoramuses whose knowledge didn't extend
beyond the circumference of a beaver pelt (Merrell, 1999). Using
these greedy rogues, who prized their own interests far above
those of the province, as ambassadors, messengers, negotiators,
spies and go-betweens went against the interests of the colonies
and against common sense, argued Johnson's secretary, Peter
Wraxall:

> It surely dos [sic] not require any detail of reasoning to evince
> how important the Capacity & Integrity of an Interpreter is
> to the public.... The Interpreter ought in my opinion to have
> a handsome Salary & be a Man of Substance & Character to
> be upon Oath neither to be concerned directly nor Indirectly in
> any Indian Trade. (Wraxall, 1915: 212, 155)

Complicating things further was the fact that the English saw
the learning of inferior tongues to be beneath their dignity
as gentlemen (Johnson was the exception, not the rule, and
an Irishman to boot). The fur trade, as a consequence, was
dominated by foreigners – Swedes, Dutch, French, Germans
and an occasional Pole – and, in the absence of better options,
Pennsylvania officials were forced to rely on unsavory characters like French traders Bizaillon and Le Tort, who, in between
their appearances as interpreters, were repeatedly investigated
on suspicion of treason and abuse of Indian trade. So narrow
was the pool of qualified interpreters in the early colonies that
even a few women squeaked through, among them Hilletie van
Olinda, daughter of a Dutch trader and a Mohawk woman,

who served as official interpreter in New York in the 1690s; Madame Bizaillon, who helped Philadelphia officials interview two Onondaga Indians in 1704; Alice Kirk, sworn as interpreter from English into Delaware in the Philadelphia Court House in 1722; and Madame Montour, a French Indian woman who worked for New York's governor Robert Hunter and then for his Pennsylvania counterpart, Patrick Gordon, helping him communicate with a delegation of the Iroquois in 1727. Shortly after, Philadelphia officials found a man they could trust.

Born in 1696 in Württemberg, Conrad Weiser was 14 when he arrived in New York with his widowed father, his siblings and other migrants from the Palatinate, sponsored as a group by Queen Anne of England. Eager to start farming, they moved to the sparsely populated Schoharie Valley, the land of the Mohawks. Conrad's father helped broker the deal and when a friendly chief invited his son to stay with the tribe and learn its tongue, he agreed – the settlers could use an interpreter and he would have one less mouth to feed. Young Conrad, eager to get away from his detested stepmother, didn't object either, but his eight-month stay wasn't all fun. "I suffered much from the excessive cold, for I was but badly clothed," recalled Weiser later, "and towards spring also from hunger, for the Indians had nothing to eat" (Weiser, 1853: 2). Still, he did develop an affection for the people and would stay in touch with his adoptive family for the rest of his life. He also made good progress in the language and perfected his skills upon his return:

An English mile from my father's house there lived several Maqua [Mohawk] families and there were always Maquas among us hunting, so that there was always something for me to do in interpreting, but without pay! There was no one else to be found among our people who understood the language, so I gradually became completely master of the language, so far as my years and other circumstances permitted. (Weiser, 1853: 3)

The governor of New York, meanwhile, was piqued that the Germans had moved into Schoharie Valley without his consent and, as squabbles over land escalated, some Palatines turned to Pennsylvania, whose governor invited them to settle in the fertile valley of Tulpehocken. In 1729, Conrad Weiser, who by then was married and had four children, followed his country-men there and became a prosperous farmer and businessman, a schoolmaster and a lay reader at the Lutheran Church. At about the same time, another newcomer arrived in the nearby town of Shamokin – a quiet, diplomatic and far-sighted Oneida chief named Shikellamy, sent by the Iroquois Confederacy, known as the Six Nations, to keep an eye on Pennsylvania's Indian affairs. The white man who spoke Mohawk attracted his attention and the timing of their meeting couldn't have been better, for there was a crisis brewing in Tulpehocken, which, as it turned out, was still owned by the Delaware, the tribe that originally owned all of Pennsylvania's land and sold it bit by bit to William Penn and his successors. Conrad Weiser and his neighbors turned out to be nothing but squatters.

To maintain peace on the frontier, the Council of Pennsyl-vania reached out to the Six Nations, who claimed authority over the Delaware. Shikellamy took their message to the Iroquois capital of Onondaga and, on return, asked his new friend to accompany him to Philadelphia as an interpreter. In December 1731, Weiser made his first appearance in the capital, impressing everyone with his countenance, knowledge and skills. The next year, he was invited back to assist with negotiations between the Six Nations and the proprietor of Pennsylvania, Thomas Penn. The treaty was deemed a success and the interpreter "extremely serviceable." The chiefs, who had had unfortunate experiences with other interpreters, also took a liking to Weiser and told colonial officials "that they had found Conrad faithfull & honest; that he is a true good Man, & had spoke their Words & our Words and not his own" (*Minutes of the Provincial Council of Pennsylvania*, 1851: vol. 4, p. 88). From then on, they wanted all negotiations to be handled by Shikellamy and Weiser.

For the next three decades, "Honest Conrad" juggled his responsibilities to his family and farm with his duties as a justice of the peace and his obligations as a government advisor on Indian affairs and as Provincial Interpreter. Successful in preserv-ing the poetic nature of Indian oratory in English (his second tongue!), Weiser was also very thorough: when, at one council in Philadelphia, he and another interpreter disagreed about the meaning of a part of a Seneca chief's speech, the two arranged a meeting with the Indians to settle on the "true interpretation," which Weiser delivered the next day.

He also had to be brave. To mend and brighten the "Chain of Friendship" between the colonists and the Iroquois, Weiser had to make numerous trips to Onondaga. His travel journals – a private one in German and an official one in English – reveal the perils faced by the intrepid go-between as he hiked through the rugged landscape, waded through snow, navigated treacherous rapids and swollen streams, climbed over slippery craggy rocks, and withstood the perils of starvation, freezing cold, debilitating sickness and endless fatigue (at one point, Weiser was so worn out that he collapsed, ready to die, until Shikellamy compelled him to move on).

The high point of his career was the 1744 Treaty at Lancaster, where Maryland and Virginia joined Pennsylvania in an alliance with the Six Nations. The Mohawks did not attend and, as an honor, Weiser was invited to sign the Maryland deed on their behalf, using the new name bestowed on him by the Six Nations, Tarachiawagon, "Holder of the Heavens."

In 1758, following the French–Indian War, Weiser helped colonial authorities broker a peace agreement. When the Delaware chief Teedyuscung blamed the war on the dispossession of his people, his interpreter rendered the lament literally, presenting the chief as "a Person Sitt on a Twig." The printed version, edited by Weiser, had a more poignant opening: "I sit here as a Bird on a Bow [bough]; I look about and do not know where to go." The old pro also knew when to sit still: when the Iroquois produced an angry rant against the Delaware, he refused to interpret it, giving the aggrieved parties time to cool down and save face.

Two years later, Weiser passed away. "He was a very honest useful Man," wrote Thomas Penn upon learning the news, "and I think it will be long before we find another equal to him" (cited in Wallace, 1945: 572). His Indian allies felt the same way. At the Easton treaty of 1761, Conrad's old friend Seneca George said to Philadelphia officials: "We, the seven Nations, and our Cousins are at a great loss, and sit in darkness, as well as you, by the death of Conrad Weiser, as since his death we cannot so well understand one another" (*Minutes of the Provincial Council of Pennsylvania*, 1851: vol. 8, p. 631).

Shikellamy's son, less aggrieved, would later call Honest Conrad one of the greatest thieves of land in the world, and with some reason: in the course of his long career, Weiser facilitated 15 major land treaties and numerous minor deals with the Iroquois Confederacy that sold Delaware lands on behalf of the tribe. The museum on Weiser's estate – possibly the only museum in the world dedicated to an interpreter – unflinchingly exposes the moral and ethical contradictions of his career as mediator and ambassador of peace. It also reminds us that some cultural victories are no victories at all: accommodated by interpreters, the Delaware ended up dispossessed, betrayed by the Iroquois. Today, Pennsylvania contains no tribal lands.

References

Merrell, J. (1999) *Into the American Woods: Negotiators on the Pennsylvania Frontier*. New York: Norton.

Minutes of the Provincial Council of Pennsylvania from the organization to the termination of the proprietary government (MPCP) (1851) Harrisburg: Theo Fenn & Co.

O'Callaghan, E. (ed.) (1849) *Documentary History of the State of New York*. Albany, NY: Weed, Parsons & Co.

O'Callaghan, E. (ed.) (1856) *Documents Relative to the Colonial History of the State of New York, Procured in Holland, England and France, Volume 7*. Albany, NY: Weed, Parsons & Co.

Wallace, P. (1945) *Conrad Weiser, Friend of Colonist and Mohawk*. Philadelphia, PA: University of Pennsylvania Press.

Weiser, C. (1853) *Narrative of a Journey from Tulpehocken, in Pennsylvania, to Onondago, the Headquarters of the Six Nations of Indians Made in 1737 by Conrad Weiser*. Philadelphia, PA: John Pennington.

Wraxall, P. (1915) *An Abridgment of the Indian Affairs: Contained in Four Folio Volumes, Transacted in the Colony of New York, from the Year 1678 to the Year 1751*. Cambridge, MA: Harvard University Press.

Daniel

by Maya Muratov

On January 11, 1929, a short note announcing the death of
Daniel Z. Noorian, "archaeologist, linguist and art collector,"
appeared in the East Coast newspapers. He had passed away
the night before, in his home in Newark, New Jersey, from a
sudden heart attack. He was 65 years old. Some of the obitu-
aries mentioned his archaeological work in Babylonia and his
extensive travels in Mesopotamia. Others referred to him as an
"art expert" with galleries in New York City. His tombstone in
Rosedale Cemetery in Montclair, New Jersey, commissioned by
his wife, is decorated with stylized trees of life, a common Near
Eastern motif, and presents him to the world as "archaeologist, explorer and art collector." Indeed, he participated in the
excavations of ancient Nippur (modern-day Iraq), he travelled
frequently, and collected countess antiquities, which he sold in
his galleries. However, his successful career of an antiquarian
in the US owed much to the connections he made in his youth
while working as a dragoman, an interpreter and guide, and an
excavation foreman for several American archaeologists.

Daniel Zado Noorian was born on March 18, in either 1865
or 1866, to an Armenian family in the small city of Sert (Siirt) in
the Ottoman Empire. He was raised in this multilingual milieu
speaking Armenian, Turkish, and Arabic. It is not known when
and how he learned English, but he must have been relatively
fluent by the time he was 18 years old. It was then, in 1884, in
Constantinople, that he met Reverend Dr. William H. Ward, the
director of the Wolfe Expedition, the first American expedition
to the Near East. This contact proved instrumental for Noorian's
further career. The expedition's main purpose was to conduct
a preliminary survey, to photograph potential dig sites, and to

assess further possibilities for organizing full archaeological in-
vestigations. From the official expedition reports and Dr. Ward's
diary, Daniel Noorian emerges as an able negotiator and practical
assistant. The small American team had to constantly interact
with the natives (such as Arabs involved in archaeological digs,
sheikhs, numerous tourist guides, etc.) and, in many cases, this
was possible only through Noorian's mediation. Being fluent
in Arabic, he could easily communicate with the local Arabs,
whereas his Turkish was essential in dealing with the Ottoman
authorities (whose officials usually did not speak Arabic).
Hidden tensions and open conflicts, between various Arab clans,
between Turkish authorities and the natives, between Christians,
Muslims, and everyone in between, also had to be taken into
account. Thus, as someone with an intimate understanding of
the complex ethnic situation in the region, Noorian knew how
to engage with people of different confessions and of different
ethnicities, and often advised the Americans on how to behave,
serving as a cultural guide of sorts. Daniel's responsibilities,
however, went far beyond those of an interpreter and mediator:
he was a bodyguard, companion, manager; he was in charge
of procuring and hiring horses and boats, as well as arranging
accommodation for the team. In the course of the expedition,
Dr. Ward and Noorian seem to have become very friendly. Daniel
later moved to America, most probably at Dr. Ward's suggestion
and with his help. He first entered the US in August 1885 on
board the SS *Waesland*, crossing via Glasgow and Antwerp.
Upon his arrival, young Daniel stayed with Ward and his family
in Newark, New Jersey. While we lack any information on what
education, if any, Noorian had received at home, once in the US
he enrolled at Rutgers Preparatory School in New Brunswick.
He graduated in 1888 and immediately returned to the Near
East as part of a University of Pennsylvania expedition.

The Babylonian Expedition was sent out to excavate the site
of ancient Nippur in Mesopotamia. The first two campaigns
took place in 1888–1889 and 1889–1890, and Daniel served as
interpreter and foreman. When he joined the team, his duties
immediately turned out to be much more extensive than initially
expected. Noorian often gave the director of the dig advice on
local customs, behavior, and rules of hospitality. In addition to

translating official documents and letters, he was charged with many vital, if somewhat random, basic tasks, such as rearing gazelles for meat. When the members of the expedition travelled around, Noorian had to arrange the armed escorts or, on more than one occasion, armed with a Winchester, act as a bodyguard himself. He also had to arrange for transportation and accommodation for the team. However, one of his most important responsibilities was communicating with the workmen. In his published reports, our only source describing the situation in detail, the head of the expedition repeatedly praised Noorian for his talent and efficiency in dealing with the workmen. Indeed, as foreman, Noorian was responsible for selecting and hiring men from among the local tribes. Most importantly, however, he had to organize, direct, and generally instruct them, making sure that they would do the required work properly. As such, Noorian often had to assume the role of an informer, listening to the Arab workmen talking amongst themselves and passing on information to the director. His position was liminal and quite complex, as he belonged neither with the few American team members, nor with the local workmen. Yet, he had to maintain the balance and keep both camps happy. An instructive story, perhaps somewhat ironically told from the American perspective, illustrates this quite well. One night, as Noorian lay awake by the fire, unable to sleep due to a toothache, he heard some of the workmen discussing some of the expeditionary equipment rather too enthusiastically. He immediately informed the director of the dig, thus preventing the theft of the equipment. After this incident, the workmen assumed that the members of the expedition possessed magical powers. Having learned of this, Noorian and the director decided to reinforce this belief and one day, after a donkey belonging to the expedition was stolen and the thief refused to confess, the two organized a small but eye-catching and loud fireworks display in the middle of the night. As they had suggested to the workmen that all goods stolen from them or from their men would bring a curse on the guilty, the fireworks were taken by the unsuspecting Arab workmen as a sign of their magical ability to make stars fall from the heavens. The desired effect was soon achieved, and the culprit confessed. Noorian is repeatedly credited by the

Americans with figuring out the right approach to take with the workmen at Nippur by keeping them constantly in good humor, while at the same time maintaining vigilant surveillance. He stimulated them with little competitions in the trenches while awakening their interest by explaining what exactly they were excavating. In order to foster closer relationships, he would spend some leisure time with the workmen, sitting by the fire at night and encouraging the sheikh to tell stories. Being a Christian, he also used to spend time reading the Quran with Obeid, the son of a local *mullah*, a mosque leader. Another essential set of Noorian's duties might be best described as public relations – linguistic and cultural mediation between the Americans and various representatives of the neighboring Arab tribes, who frequently visited the camp and demanded money or guns, and occasionally threatened the team.

Towards the end of the second campaign, Noorian evidently became more of a companion to the director, who consulted him on many issues and often took his advice. Noorian's contract expired at the end of the second Nippur campaign, and having visited his home in Sert, he returned to the US "to put the experience acquired in two expeditions to practical use, as a dealer in antiquities." Most likely, this idea had sprouted in Noorian's head when he moved to the US in 1885 after the Wolfe Expedition, if not earlier. While travelling with the Babylonian Expedition, Noorian often used his time in the various cities they visited or passed through to meet up with dealers, to sample their offerings, and to acquire objects as well, both on behalf of the members of the expedition and for his own growing collection. He also undertook short reconnaissance trips to build up his growing network of dealers that would ensure a continuous supply of antiquities.

When Noorian returned to America from Nippur in 1890, he became a naturalized American citizen in October of that year and continued to reside with Dr. Ward and his two sisters on Abington Avenue in Newark. Evidently, this connection with the Wards remained quite strong and they became his adopted American family. Hetta L.H. Ward, Dr. Ward's unmarried artist sister, signed Daniel's preserved passport application from 1899, as a witness. It also seems that Noorian developed quite an attachment to this neighborhood as, several years later, he bought himself a house on the very same street – 60 Abington Avenue. He was to reside in that house for the rest of his life. Such is the story of Daniel Zado Noorian, an interpreter turned antiquities dealer with galleries on Fifth Avenue in New York, whose first important jobs were as an interpreter helping two American archaeological teams navigate the uncertain waters of the multilingual and multicultural Ottoman Empire in the last quarter of the 19th century.

Darko

by Stefanie Meier

In many ways, medical interpreting is an ideal profession for Darko. The flexibility allows him to maintain his free and at times lazy attitude to life; it provides him with the opportunity to follow his many interests apart from the necessity of wage labor. Darko works as freelance interpreter for the Christian Solidarity Fund (CSF), which brokers interpreting professionals for consultations in hospitals and private practices. His schedule is extremely flexible, and every week looks different. At times, he juggles too many appointments, while at others, he is in need of additional engagements to reach the amount of money needed by the end of the month. Darko receives text messages or phone calls ahead of any possible engagement, sometimes many days or weeks in advance, but sometimes with emergency requests only a few hours before the work opportunity. It is in moments like these that he might feel obliged to accept a request in order to remain on the list of desirable interpreters. Apart from his work, he participates in talks and workshops organized by the CSF, working towards a certificate for intercultural interpreting. Darko's carefree attitude and his distracted personality help him remain aloof of the insecurity that accompanies such a flexible work arrangements. However, the hectic and irregular schedule also holds the danger of him losing his good reputation or even his job because he forgets appointments from time to time.

Darko has been my close friend for more than 10 years. A few years ago I asked him if he could imagine becoming a research participant in a project on the role of language in the Swiss healthcare marketplace. He agreed. Medical interpreting is not Darko's passion. He started this type of work around five years before we first interviewed him. He decided to follow this work opportunity in order to financially support himself during the last months of writing his PhD in philosophy. Darko is originally from a small town close to Belgrade, where he grew up, studied and later started his dissertation. He came to Switzerland for a university exchange and to improve his German skills. He had learned the language back in high school and continued with German at university because of his engagement with German philosophy, primarily focusing on Hegel, Kant and Marx. In some ways, medical interpreting was a stressful profession at that moment in his life: it was difficult to stay concentrated and write while repeatedly checking his phone for new engagements or rushing off to an appointment in the middle of the day. On the other hand, his work with the CSF was by far the most lucrative of his side jobs in Switzerland. His limited writing skills in German did not allow him to do administrative jobs and he was completely untalented at (and uninterested in) manual labor. Thus, choices were limited. He had worked as a night porter at a mid-range hotel, as a guard at a gallery for contemporary art and, occasionally, as a Serbian teacher. Medical interpreting paid him about twice the hourly wage he had earned in these positions.

Much in his life has changed since. Darko faced the denial of his visa after finishing his doctoral thesis. Therefore, he had to marry his partner, despite their opposition to marriage as an institution perpetuating patriarchy and capitalism. He arranged for his younger brother to join him in Switzerland as the prospect of finding work in rural Serbia was non-existent. Then, Darko became a father. These new responsibilities could have changed his carefree nature but, fortunately, they did not, at least not substantially. Darko, his partner, his daughter and his brother share a flat, which is just one of the units in a further collectively organized house. They share not only their experience with 'Fortress Europe' and the difficulty of gaining access to the Swiss German labor market, but also a similar anti-capitalist, anti-consumerist worldview. It is this outlook on life, which comes with fewer expenses and a bigger social network that practices mutual aid, along with the cheap rent, that allows Darko to be relaxed about his precarious working conditions. His wage from medical interpreting, which takes about 16 hours of his time per week, is high enough to provide his share of the collective's economic needs.

Although Darko's work as an interpreter is not his passion, he enjoys analyzing the systemic oppression he witnesses during the encounters, reflecting on the exploitation of his labor and negotiating his own problematic role as a facilitator. An episode occurring as Darko was interpreting for one patient, Ratko, during a doctor's appointment, revealed such a moment of tension that arose from parallels and clashes between the life trajectories of the interpreter and the patient. Ratko originally came to Switzerland from Bosnia and was required to undergo a regular medical re-evaluation of his claim for a disability pension. The re-evaluation at which Darko was interpreting mainly consisted of a question-and-answer exercise between the doctor and Ratko. After five minutes, Ratko broke down in tears as his tragic life story unfolded. The 50-year-old patient, who looked many years older, spoke about his life of hard work in a Swiss factory. A work accident had made him incapable of continuing his contract and his wife had also lost her job. Now they were struggling with growing depression. His son, who looked tired after a night shift, was accompanying him. He was in his mid-20s, lived with his parents and was working multiple jobs as a security guard and in pizza delivery. Darko shares Ratko's working-class background but, unlike Ratko's son, grew up in communist Yugoslavia, which allowed him to go to university. He could delve into philosophy, came to Switzerland as a doctoral student with excellent German reading skills and the craftiness needed to juggle his economic responsibilities with as little effort as possible. Darko stoically interpreted all that he could possibly comprehend. He turned sobs and moaning into words and sentences, fragments of Serbo-Croat, Swiss German and German into a sad narration of underpaid work, depression and chronic diseases. Darko remained calm, asked Ratko follow-up questions, helped him decipher lists of medications he was taking and eventually seemed to have won the trust and respect of all involved.

This shows that Darko is an ideal medical interpreter. His language skills and profound knowledge of medical terminology make him a central figure in the local healthcare industry, whom stakeholders can capitalize on. It is this moral dilemma of being part of an oppressive system that weighs heavily on Darko. He knows full well how often patients' wishes are denied. They depend on the credibility of their story, the acknowledgment of their bad health in order to keep their pensions or avoid deportation. He listens to their stories, sometimes advises them on their best chances and translates their narratives, which become fragments in the surveillance machinery. He can relate to their stories because of his own experiences, or because of his political and philosophical reflections. Still, he must transmit them as required by the system, knowing of the futility and powerlessness of his position.

However, this moral dilemma notwithstanding, Darko's work arrangement gives him time to follow his true passions: philosophy, music and, since her birth, the raising of his daughter. His passion for discovering and collecting music has led to the formation of a DJ collective. This group organizes events and concerts that combine music and political education. As an academically trained philosopher, he is also engaged in the creation of a non-commercial and non-authoritative space for knowledge production. This way of sharing and producing knowledge corresponds more fully to his political convictions than academia. However, his résumé also does not allow him to continue his academic career (in Switzerland); the many years of developing his dissertation and his non-existent publication record in German do not go well with a university labor market that increasingly counts points and articles. Neither does a working-class background in Serbia. However, I know how exceptional Darko is at teaching and doing research and I could see what a central figure he is in a philosophical circle in Serbia. But while I grow wildly angry at the limitations that come with a non-linear life trajectory and a foreign passport, Darko stays calm. Medical interpreting gives him the opportunity strictly to separate necessary wage labor and the passion for knowledge production. This decision of his resonates with my own situation in life as a researcher with doubts about where to find important spaces for knowledge production. This shared outlook on the need or wish to separate wage labor from other activities structures my own perception of how medical interpreting shapes Darko's life. The fragility that comes with such a life arrangement, however, becomes clear in moments where just one of the elements changes: pressure and insecurity were sharply raised when the old landlord declared his intention to profitably sell the old house Darko and his collective were living in. Darko himself might have chosen to highlight different aspects of his experience with interpretation; he probably would have inserted a more systemic, anti-capitalist analysis. But he enjoyed reading this, my interpretation, because of the interplay of his work arrangement and his passions in life.

Enrique

by Carla M. Pacis

On August 10, 1519, Portuguese explorer Ferdinand Magellan
set sail from Spain to discover a western sea route to the Spice
Islands for King Carlos I. In 15th- and 16th-century Europe,
spices like nutmeg and cloves were much sought-after com-
modities in the same way that oil is today. They were used to
preserve food, particularly meat, and enhance flavor. Carlos
I granted Magellan five ships for this significant voyage. On
board Magellan's own ship, the *Trinidad*, was his personal slave
Enrique, a young man of Malay descent.

By the time Magellan sailed for the Spice Islands, he had
already sailed to most of the Portuguese territories in the New
World, including what is now Malaysia. In Malacca, he bought
a young slave boy, had him baptized Enrique and brought him
to Portugal, hence his name, Enrique de Malacca. While living
in Portugal, Enrique learned to speak Portuguese to be able to
communicate with his master, his master's family and everyone
else in his new world.

The earliest documentation of Enrique's existence is in
the chronicles of Magellan's voyage by Antonio Pigafetta. He
is referred to as a slave. According to Magellan's will, Enrique
was born in Malacca. In fact, there is a statue of him in the
Maritime Museum of Malacca. The museum aims to highlight Malacca's importance as a sultanate and as a Portuguese,
Dutch and British colony. One of its exhibits is a replica of the
Portuguese galleon *Flor de la Mar*, which sank off the coast
of Malacca. In his chronicles, Pigafetta surmised that Enrique
had been captured by slave raiders from Sumatra and sold on
the slave market in Malacca. It can also be argued that Enrique
may instead have been born in Sugbu or what is now known as

Cebu in the Philippines, as the eminent Filipino historian Carlos Quirino claims. We know that Enrique could either understand and speak the different languages of these two areas, or he knew a common trade language that was spoken. It is believed that the latter is more probable.

By accident, on March 16, 1521, Magellan found himself in Philippine waters, rather than the Spice Islands or the Moluccas in the Indonesian archipelago. Shortly after they had anchored off a breakwater, a flotilla of large boats sailed out to meet the Spanish galleons, *Trinidad*, *Victoria*, *Santiago*, *Concepcion* and *San Antonio*. The men in the boats called out to the men in the ships in a language that, luckily for him, only Enrique understood. From that day on, Enrique assumed the important role of interpreter, allowing for many interactions to transpire between Magellan and the rajahs he met over the four weeks he spent in Sugbu, shortly before his death. Enrique's first task as interpreter was to request food for his master, the chronicler, the priest, the ship captains and the rest of the crews on all five ships.

The man on the first boat, whom Pigafetta described as being draped in gold, was a local *Datu* (chieftain), Humabon. He developed a complex and controversial relationship with Magellan. Humabon even asked his wife, Humamay, to convert to Catholicism, in all probability influenced by Enrique and his own desire for Spanish help against his rival, Datu Lapu-Lapu of Mactan, whose holdings he coveted. Although the interpreter's role is to strictly and accurately communicate what is being said, it would not be far-fetched to assume that Enrique may have given or was even asked for his personal opinions, as he was familiar with both worlds.

Instead of sailing on to the Spice Islands, Magellan decided to stay in Sugbu in the hopes of finding gold to make up for the spices he had not found and in order to conquer the rest of the islands in the name of the King of Spain and convert their people to the Catholic faith. Magellan's prolonged presence suited Humabon very well, as he was very interested in the firearms the Spaniards had brought, which he could use against Lapu-Lapu.

Magellan met many more *Datus* (they are listed by Pigafetta), always with Enrique acting as interpreter. He went along with his master's political maneuverings with the *Datus* and had a hand in arranging the blood compact, or *casi-casi*, between Magellan and Datus Humabon, Awi and Kolambu. This meant that Magellan would protect these *Datus*, and they him.

Eventually, Humabon was able to convince Magellan, through Enrique, to attack Lapu-Lapu of Mactan, and it was in this ill-advised skirmish that Magellan met his death on April 27, 1521. He was hit by a poison arrow in the leg and left to die by his retreating crew. His death meant, according to Magellan's will, that Enrique was now a free man:

> And by this my present will and testament, I declare and ordain as free and quit of every obligation of captivity, subjection, and slavery, my captured slave Enrique, mulatto, native of the city of Malacca, of the age of twenty-six years more or less, that from the day of my death thenceforward ... and I desire that of my estate there may be given to the said Enrique the sum of ten thousand maravedis in money for his support; and this manumission I grant because he is a Christian, and that he may pray to God for my soul....

But Enrique's story does not end here.

The new leader of the expedition, Juan Serrano, refused to acknowledge Magellan's will and grant Enrique his freedom. He wanted Enrique to sail with the remaining crew back to Spain. Enrique refused, and his last act as interpreter was to secure his freedom.

Enrique convinced Humabon that the Spaniards had plans to kidnap him and bring him to Spain. Furious, Humabon organized a feast for the Spaniards where, at a given moment, his men would attack and kill them. Pigafetta, who was nursing a wound to the cheek as a result of the skirmish with Lapu-Lapu, stayed on one of the remaining ships, along with others who were wounded; they were joined by those who returned early from the feast, feeling a certain unease. Humabon gave the signal and the Spaniards who remained at the feast were massacred, including Juan Serrano. It is after this massacre that Enrique received another appellation: El Negro, or 'the Black One', referring either simply to the color of his skin, or to his alleged involvement in the massacre. It is also here that Enrique's story ends from the point of view of Western history.

Under the leadership of Sebastian Elcano, the Spaniards sailed away from Sugbu as fast as they could in the two remaining ships – the *Trinidad* and the *Victoria*. It can only be assumed that Enrique, no longer slave or interpreter, was now truly a free man, finally living again among his own people.

Contemporary historians and writers from the Philippines and Malaysia have written about Enrique, with each country claiming him as their own. A children's book by Reni Roxas and Marc Singer and a young-adult novel on Enrique written by myself were published shortly after an article by Carlos Quirino about him appeared in the *Philippines Free Press* magazine in 1991. In 2021, the Philippines will be celebrating Ferdinand Magellan's 'discovery' of the Philippines 500 years ago. Already, articles on Enrique have been surfacing in print and digital media. It is only a matter of time before our intrepid interpreter will take center stage alongside his former master.

Print sources

Bergeen, L. (2002) *Over the Edge of the World: Magellan's Terrifying Circumnavigation of the Globe*. New York: William Morrow.

Pigafetta, A. (1995) *The First Voyage Around the World (1519–1522): An Account of Magellan's Expedition*. New York: Marsillio Publishers.

Quirino, C. (1991) The first man around the world was a Filipino. *Philippines Free Press*, 28 December.

Online resources

Caryl-Sue. "April 27, 1521CE: Magellan Killed in Philippine Skirmish", National Geographic Society, April 11, 2014, https://www.national geographic.org/thisday/apr27/magellan-killed-philippine-skirmish/

"Ferdinand Magellan: Facts and Biography", amp.livescience.com, http://www.softschools.com/facts/biography/ferdinand_magellan_facts/848/

"Magellan's Expedition Circumnavigates the Globe", History, A&E Television Networks, 21 July 2010, https://www.history.com/this-day-in-history/magellans-expedition-circumnavigates-globe

Evans

by Carmen Delgado Luchner

There are thousands of organizations currently implementing 'development projects' in Kenya. Most of these projects aim to improve access to water, healthcare, or education for people who live in poverty. Some involve building schools or providing books and uniforms for children; others focus on training members of the population in basic healthcare. These projects bring together very different groups of people: Kenyan and international aid workers, community elders, farmers and the urban poor. In the framework of my research, I interviewed 15 Kenyan workers employed by non-governmental organizations (NGOs) to find out how they implement participatory development approaches with beneficiaries who do not speak English. I gradually realized that all of these development professionals were also regularly interpreting or relying on someone else's interpretation. Evans' story is paradigmatic, and his[1] account is based on the experiences of all these NGO workers and their different organizations.

As a Kenyan NGO worker, Evans interacts with the local community and with NGO workers from Europe or North America. He works for a Catholic NGO based in the capital, Nairobi. However, he spends about half of his time in rural areas, in order to interact with those whom development jargon still generally refers to as 'beneficiaries'.

Interpreting is going on at every step of the way in Kenyan development projects. There are so many interactions that involve translation: NGO workers have to translate local needs into fundable projects, translate development jargon so that non-experts can understand it and, very often, translate or interpret from one language to another. All Kenyan staff I encountered had done it at one time or another, often without being fully aware of it. The language mediation part of their job is invisible; it is implicit and taken for granted. There is no budget line for translation, no specific planning, no monitoring and evaluation, no real in-depth discussion about it. Interpreting just happens, based on immediate needs. Today Evans will be the interpreter; tomorrow he will rely on someone else's interpretation.

Evans works with many partner organizations from Europe and America, who help his NGO in obtaining funding for their projects. The Kenyan NGO then has to send these partners regular updates about their progress, including feedback from the local community. Evans does not remember anyone from a partner organization ever asking how he manages to get this feedback in English. Maybe their international partners do not know that many people in Kenya do not speak English, because they only interact with Evans and his colleagues. Or they just assume that their Kenyan counterparts speak the languages of all beneficiaries and somehow make it work.

Based on the reports their partners send them from Kenya, these international NGOs, based in the Global North, then publish stories on their websites and in leaflets, writing things like, '"The project really helped me improve my approach and increase the yield of my dairy farm" (Nyambura, 45, from Limuru)' or, '"I am so happy that I was able to participate in the vocational training programme and start my own business as a tailor. Now my daughters can go to school" (Kipchoge, 32 from Eldoret)'. But Nyambura and Kipchoge do not speak English, so they never said those words. At best, their words were translated faithfully and transmitted to the foreign partner in English. In other cases, the statements attributed to them are just extrapolations from a much more general project report. When we read those little beneficiary stories, we are reading the result of work done by someone like Evans, and yet we feel that we are connecting directly with Nyambura and Kipchoge.

Evans is not an interpreter, but his job often requires him to interpret. Project beneficiaries are mainly rural populations, and the older members of the community might be illiterate and speak neither English nor Swahili. The success of a development project often depends on the active participation of its beneficiaries. To make sure that their views are taken into account,

Kenyan NGO staff collect feedback from beneficiaries through questionnaires or moderated group discussions. Part of Evans' job when collecting this feedback consists in helping beneficiaries to understand the questions and ensuring that their comments are reflected in the report that he will draft in English.

When beneficiaries speak Swahili or Evans' own mother tongue, he usually interprets the questions for them and then writes a summary of their answers in English. Evans knows the projects very well, so even if the answers from beneficiaries are not clear, he is usually very confident that he knows what beneficiaries meant to say, and writes that down. In most cases, beneficiaries cannot read the written summary Evans produces, so if they want to know what is being written down, he has to translate it back for them.

In some cases, collecting feedback is a very difficult task, especially when working with a community of beneficiaries with whom Evans shares no common language. In these situations, he has to rely on a member of the community to interpret, as there are usually a few people who can at least speak Swahili, if not English. In these situations Evans loses his role as translator and becomes a consumer of someone else's translation. This can be quite tedious because the interpretation might not be accurate. Trust is very important in this context, so NGO workers prefer the interpreter to be someone from within the community. That way, they have a stake in the project, and the NGO workers can be sure that they will do their best to make the meeting successful.

It is interesting to hear Evans discuss the insider status of the interpreters, as it clashes with professional understandings of interpreter impartiality. In the Kenyan development NGOs I studied, interpreters are generally invisible, not because they are impartial, but because they are so partial that they become indistinguishable from the other participants in a meeting, except when they open their mouths to interpret.

Usually, several beneficiaries or members of the community can also speak at least a little bit of English or Swahili. If they think the translator made a mistake, they will object to his translation, in some cases even coercing him into translating correctly. When necessary, NGOs use double translation. For example, if Evans goes to the field with an international visitor and the community members speak in their mother tongue and their own interpreter then puts it into Swahili, Evans will translate into English for the foreigner.

Another instance of interpretation occurs during workshops, for example awareness-raising about HIV/AIDS or infant mortality. When Evans facilitates these workshops, his training materials are all written in English, because the NGO uses the same materials all over the country and sometimes even develops them in collaboration with partners from other countries in East Africa. But Evans has to then give the workshop orally, in Swahili or in the local language, which means he sometimes struggles to get very accurate equivalents for technical or medical terms. Maybe these terms do not exist in the other language, or, even when they exist, the beneficiaries would not necessarily understand them because they do not have medical training or a high level of education. So, Evans relies a lot on images during training, at least for the materials that the beneficiaries see. Sometimes, equivalents or explanations for technical terms are coined on the spot. I am left wondering how many different words beneficiaries have heard as equivalents for the same term in English, and whether they actually know that all these are just different people's attempts to refer to exactly the same thing.

English itself is also a challenge in Evans' work. Some community members will understand it, as long as it is spoken by a Kenyan or in the way Kenyans usually speak. The accent of British or American visitors can be very challenging for beneficiaries. Evans is livid as he explains that some of the NGO workers from the US or the UK seem to have received a kind of 'sensitivity training' before they come to Kenya, where they are told to speak slowly, use simple words and articulate clearly. The problem is that they do this even when speaking to Evans and his colleagues, not only to the beneficiaries! Evans perceives this as extremely condescending, while the beneficiaries often do not understand them either way. And yet, simple English or 'broken Swahili' is routinely used by Kenyan NGO workers to talk to beneficiaries.

Whether Evans can speak the local language of a community his organization works with is often a matter of coincidence.

When Evans was recruited, nobody asked him about his language skills. The advertisement just specified that excellent English was a requirement. That is usually the case for any office job in Kenya, whether or not it involves close collaboration with international partners. But in most office jobs, people do not interact with people from slums or remote villages, so English is enough. In Evans' case, not even Swahili was mentioned as a requirement, even though it is the main language he now uses when interacting with colleagues and communities.

Of course, by looking at Evans' last name, any Kenyan can tell what his mother tongue is and will assume that he can speak that language: in Kenya, language can never be separated from tribe. So, if an NGO publishes a job advertisement specifying that it wants someone who speaks Gikuyu, or Dholuo, or Kalenjin, that would imply it wants to recruit someone from a specific ethnic group. This is a red line, since Kenya has a recent and painful history of intra-ethnic violence. Therefore, anything that would indicate favoritism towards members of one group could easily spark tension. Most NGOs based in Nairobi end up employing mainly those who live in the capital, and the majority of them speak Gikuyu. For positions in rural areas, they usually advertise for 'someone from the area' or 'someone from the community' instead of specifying that they need someone who speaks the language. That way, the message is still clear, but they do not break the taboo of advertising by tribe.

The downside of rendering language all but invisible during recruitment is that the makeup of an organization's staff does not always match its beneficiaries. Evans remembers working with beneficiaries from his own community only once and recalls how pleasant it was. Communication was smooth and direct, and Evans felt that he understood the community at a much deeper level and really felt their concerns. Since then, whenever Evans has to interpret, his aim is to get this same feeling across to his listeners.

Note

(1) 'Evans' is a pseudonym used to represent the entirety of my interviewees. Since the majority of interviewees (8 out of 15) were male,

the pronouns he/him/his are used throughout this text to ensure read-ability and avoid confusion, as them/their is often used to refer to other stakeholders.

Fatima

by Inmaculada García-Sánchez

Fatima was nine and a half years old when I first met her in a pediatrician's office at the local clinic, although her petite figure made her seem younger. Her small build and a face still closer to that of a girl than of a tween made jarring the relative ease and poise with which she was handling the complex demands of simultaneous medical interpreting: work that children are usually neither allowed to do nor considered capable of doing competently (at least in child-centered, late capitalist societies). Children are not typically heard authoritatively in such institutional spaces, much less the children of economic migrants, like Fatima, who are often thought of as having serious linguistic deficits.

Fatima, along with her peers Manal and Abdelkarim, was one of a group of Moroccan immigrant children in this southern Spanish town who seemed to have a knack for translation; children often translated for their Moroccan families and Spanish medical staff or bureaucrats, were reputedly good at it, and expressed enjoyment of the task, or at least didn't mind it. With so many adult members of Moroccan households working two, sometimes three shifts as workers on the labor-intensive farms surrounding the town, and austerity budgets slashing vulnerable interpretation services (non-essential in an assimilationist view), Moroccan immigrant families and Spanish medical/institutional staff were often forced to rely on child language brokers to perform language services key to the sustainability of communities and smooth functioning of institutions. To avoid a constant battle of wills with their own children if they were unwilling or reluctant to do it, adults often sought out children like Fatima, who thus became what we call community interpreters. Thus,

Fatima not only took care of most of her own family's interpretation needs, but was also often recruited by many other (mostly female) relatives, neighbors, and acquaintances of her parents to help with translation tasks. Mostly, she accompanied them to the town's health center for medical visits, but sometimes also assisted with paperwork, either at government offices or by translating official letters received by mail.

Fatima, who arrived in Spain with her family as a toddler, was the second youngest child in her family, having two older sisters and a four-year-old brother. Half-jokingly, I asked Fatima about her doing most of the interpreting in her home even though she was the youngest girl. She smiled a little self-consciously and shrugged, saying matter of factly a second or two later that when she went out with her mother, one of her older sisters had to stay home to take care of her brother, while her other older sister worked in the fields with their father. She said nothing of the other women who would come looking for her help. "But do you *really* like it?," I tried again, hoping to get at Fatima's own understanding of language brokering. Popular biases hold that child language brokering can bring emotional burdens and other negative psychosocial outcomes for immigrant children. I was curious, but also worried about how to phrase the question to avoid putting ideas in the young girl's head, ideas about what she was doing that may have not occurred to her otherwise. She shrugged again. She did this a lot when I asked her questions about her work as a language broker, but not because she did not know what or how to answer. Rather, it was an expression of not having thought all that much about it before.

Sometimes, she would also stare at me with her big brown eyes full of curiosity, as if wondering why I would ask so many questions about tasks that she herself considered utterly unremarkable, something she just did to "help out at home". Eventually, she lowered her voice, looking sideways furtively, as if someone other than me could hear her: it was sweeping and mopping that she did not like and was happy to get away from any time she could. She then described what sounded like feelings of self-efficacy and self-accomplishment: when she was translating, she felt content; she liked that she was able to help other people because she knew Spanish. Sometimes, she felt as if she were doing an important job. "But you *are* doing an important job," I replied, trying to underscore for her the significance of the language services that she was performing for her family and community. Now, that is an idea I did not mind reinforcing for her, particularly in the face of the many negative messages that immigrant children like Fatima receive about their supposed linguistic deficiencies.

It is perhaps not surprising that children like Fatima have only a vague awareness, if any at all, of the value of the work they do as language brokers. The common invisibilization of children's labor in general, and of immigrant children's in particular (immigrant children ironically are often depicted as economic burdens on state resources), means that many institutions rely on their labor to provide critical services without any recognition, much less any support. Even in academia, only a handful of scholars have paid serious attention to immigrant children's language brokering as labor with quantifiable, material, economic value. Fewer still have considered the essential immaterial benefits children like Fatima produce, particularly in increasingly information/knowledge-based economies. But it is precisely Fatima's ability to negotiate linguistic, sociocultural, and political boundaries in encounters characterized by inequality, through her resourceful communicative skills and affective labor, that has been most memorable for me over the years.

Let me illustrate how Fatima navigated the vulnerabilities and contradictions of her work on behalf of others by taking you back to the winter afternoon when I first had the opportunity to observe Fatima in action at the local health center. She had come with one of her neighbors and her small son, Ali, for a follow-up to a visit that had taken place a few weeks earlier. The boy was not eating well, and the growth assessment showed that he was low on the weight-for-length percentile. Both the visit and Fatima's Moroccan Arabic–Spanish simultaneous interpreting had been proceeding smoothly. The mother, however, had been complaining that she had had a lot of problems having her son take the syrup that the pediatrician had prescribed during the initial visit. As the mother responded to the doctor's various comments and suggestions, describing difficulties in getting her son to eat more nutritiously in what sounded like stressful meal interactions, her anxiety, worry, and frustration were becoming more and more evident.

During a pause in the conversation, while the doctor was comparing test results and writing a few notes in Ali's file, the mother turned to Fatima and asked her whether she spoke *tmaziRt*, one of the dialects of Amazighe: "sham tassawalad tmaziRt?" ("Do you speak tmaziRt?"). Fatima answered that she spoke a little. The mother, taking advantage of the fact that her little boy did not speak Amazighe, then asked Fatima to help her invent a scary story that would coerce the boy into eating and taking his medicine. Fatima did not respond. Instead, she stared at the mother, then lowered her head while playing with the fringes of her red woollen poncho, and finally looked up at the mother again, who was still looking at her expectantly. Perhaps assuming from Fatima's lack of a verbal response and compliance that the girl did not, after all, speak Amazighe, the mother lowered her voice slightly and switched back to Moroccan Arabic. She suggested telling Ali that the doctor would have to take rather drastic measures if he continued refusing to eat: "šufi, kolilha ila mabġaš yakol waš nrat$olhom baš takla'lo šwiya man alwadnin warras" ("Look, tell him that if he doesn't want to eat we will return for a little bit of his ears and head to be removed"). Fatima glanced back and forth hesitantly between the mother and the doctor, softly biting her lips. The doctor, who by then had finished taking her notes, also looked inquisitively at the family, waiting for a translation of what had just transpired between them. Fatima hesitated for a few seconds longer and, finally, composing herself, said to the doctor that the mother wanted to confirm whether the boy had to take the syrup for the next two months: "Dice que si tiene que tomar dos meses de esto, no?" ("She says whether he has to take two months of this, right?"). The pediatrician responded affirmatively, repeating the instructions she had given earlier in the interaction: a small dose of the syrup every day, for two months, before breakfast or lunch. Fatima turned to her neighbor and told her in Moroccan Arabic that the doctor had said the same thing about the syrup that she had said before: "kalatlak kimma kalatlak kbila" ("she has said to you like she told you before").

Soon, after a little more back and forth between the mother and the doctor, they agreed on a plan; the mother thanked the doctor, and left the office.

While not exceptional, Fatima is one of the most impressive child language brokers I have ever met, not just for her linguistic talent to *translate*, but also for her ability to negotiate, contest, and even *transcend* borders in fraught contact zones. She gives new meaning to lines in a poem by Gloria Andalzúa: "To survive the Borderlands/you must live *sin fronteras*/[you must] be a crossroads".

Google Translate

by Stefan Vollmer

Excerpt from my research diary: January 2017, Syrian Kitchen (Leeds, UK). All names are pseudonyms.

I make my way inside the Syrian Kitchen, a pay-as-you-feel café in Leeds, which is run by Syrian refugees who volunteer to cook and serve authentic Syrian food. Again, I sit with the usual suspects: Rojan, Dilara, Jino, Mary and a newly arrived Iranian man called Amin. It's hectic and noisy here today, as there's so much going on; people are constantly coming and going, sitting down and standing up; food is brought out and plates are cleared away.

I feel like I need to go somewhere else to have a quiet conversation with Rojan, who has agreed to be a participant in my ethnographic study concerning newly arrived refugees' smartphone practices. Rojan, his mother, Dilara, and his brother, Jino, have been in Leeds for only a couple of months. As we all wait for the food to arrive, we talk about how to say 'thank you' in different languages, such as Arabic, Farsi, Kurdish and Turkish. Rojan, an eager learner of English, who is fluent in Kurdish and Arabic and speaks some Turkish and Farsi too, explains that the expressions for 'thank you' in those languages share a common linguistic root.

As our shared language is English, Rojan looks up Farsi and Arabic translations of English words with the help of Google Translate, mainly to talk to Amin, the Iranian newcomer. Amin is a novice learner of English and can participate in the conversation only to a limited extent. During our meal, we keep coming back to Google Translate; Rojan explains that he always uses the app during his ESOL (English for speakers of other languages) classes, especially when his teachers use words he doesn't understand. More importantly though, Google Translate was indispensable during his journey from Syria to the UK. Rojan's journey was a very difficult and perilous one, with many detours and dead ends, leading him through Turkey, Greece, Germany and France. Whenever Rojan didn't know a word in Turkish, Greek, German, French or English, he would consult Google Translate.

Suddenly, Amin, who hasn't really been saying anything during all this, seems to be in a lot of pain. His right hand is on his heart, indicating that he's got chest pains. He takes long deep breaths. He looks pretty faint. Mary, a local volunteer English teacher and a regular to the Syrian Kitchen, who has been tutoring Rojan and Amin since their arrival in the UK, asks if he's okay. He says 'yeah, yeah', while reaching out with both of his hands, gesturing as if wanting to say 'It's nothing; don't worry, Mary'.

It is clear, though, that Amin looks in distress and needs help. Mary gets him a glass of water. Rojan speaks Arabic to him, which Amin understands to some degree. They have a brief conversation. Amin keeps repeating the same word in Farsi. After several unsuccessful attempts to understand the man, Rojan picks up his phone, opens Google Translate, types something and then explains that Amin is asking for *quarfa*, which means cinnamon.

All this happens very quickly. Everyone is slightly confused. Why would Amin want cinnamon now? A few moments later, one of the waiters comes along with a huge Tupperware box filled with ground cinnamon. Amin takes a big spoonful of cinnamon and swallows it in one go, without any water. I closely watch his face; he seems to relax as the cinnamon enters his body. Amin signals with his hands that the cinnamon slows down his heartbeat. Later, at home, I look up the effects of cinnamon on the heart. I find out that cinnamon, among other spices, is a remedy for heartburn.

After he somewhat recovers, everyone's obviously concerned, and we are all still trying to figure out what had actually happened. Rojan, who used to work as a hospital technician in Aleppo, keeps asking Amin medical questions. Amin gestures that there's something wrong with his head. I wonder if we should call an ambulance. Mary says that she thinks he might have had a heart attack. Rojan keeps asking questions and eventually consults Google Translate again. This time, the app suggests that Amin has a problem with his nerves.

This new piece of information is crucial. Mary, who has been in close contact with Amin since his arrival, tells me that he has a very important interview tomorrow, concerning his family's right for asylum in the UK. Amin is clearly afraid and worried. Still, he smiles at us, despite his nerve-wracking circumstances and despite all that cinnamon.

Things don't really go back to normal after this. Mary encourages Amin to go home to have a lie down. Next, Saad joins us. Saad manages the volunteers cooking at the Syrian Kitchen. In his hands, he holds the shopping list with the ingredients for next week's shopping. Mary and Rojan will take care of the shopping this time. The shopping list is in English, but some of the words are also in Arabic. Mary asks about one of the words. Again, Rojan uses Google Translate to negotiate between the two languages. This time, the word Mary is looking up is *kazbra* (coriander). Then, it's time to go. I say my goodbyes and I head out.

This short anecdote underscores the significance of freely accessible, synchronous mobile machine translation apps for language learners, particularly in everyday, superdiverse and multilingual contexts. Over the years, Google Translate has become a well-known app for mobile machine translations. More than 200 million people use Google Translate every day to negotiate between over 100 languages. As the app also affords users multimodal translations, for instance translations of written text, voice recordings and even photographs, Google Translate has increased in value to users with limited literacy or formal education.

More than that, as the vignette highlights, smartphone-mediated translations are deeply embedded in complex everyday practices, such as sharing a meal with friends. As the story unfolds, Rojan repeatedly integrates Google Translate to broker between multilingual speakers, thus suggesting that, particularly in urban and multilingual contexts, mobile machine translations have become deeply ingrained in everyday life. At the Syrian Kirchen, it is apparent that Google Translate touches upon aspects of life which range from the banal to the crucially important.

At the same time, Google Translate is part of Alphabet Inc., a multibillion-dollar cooperation with an audience of over one billion users. Alphabet Inc. owns many of today's most popular online platforms, including YouTube, Android and Google Maps, which all garner, store, use and sell customer data for tremendous profits. Undoubtedly, the vast reach of Alphabet Inc. and its extended network of companies benefits the app's accuracy *vis-à-vis* its translations; as part of Alphabet Inc., Google Translate has access to an unprecedented multilingual corpus, allowing it to produce ever-improving, readily available translations. On the other hand, of course, the use of the translation app, particularly in private, and at times intimate social settings, raises obvious questions about privacy, data protection and ethics. This rings particularly true in this vignette's context of mobility and migration, where newcomers of often contested legal status routinely draw on Google Translate to navigate their everyday lives. This then suggests that newly arrived migrant language learners might unwittingly release sensitive information as they rely on Google Translate to broker their daily life experiences.

Ilona

by Dina Bolokan

Literature and language had always been Ilona's points of access to the world. She decided to become a teacher. Her mother and grandmother were both teaching, too. This was in the 1980s, in Moldova, a Soviet republic. She interpreted literature with young people and reflected with them on moral questions. She saw this work as a means to prepare her students for life, to strengthen them in order to face the world out there. She loved being a teacher, which included taking her time for pupils who had difficulties outside the classroom. She guided them through growing up. Her philosophy was (and has remained) that educational work is all about giving young people the means to reflect and judge on their own, in order to become independent of adults.

Emigration took away Ilona's passion and profession, and it would be decades before she came back to this world of interpretation. Leaving her life in Moldova was hard for Ilona as I, who have been close to her, could observe over decades. Her husband had wanted nothing but to leave for a long time. For years she objected to migrating. But the crumbling of the Soviet Union frightened her. The war between Transnistria and Moldova began. It was 1990. Tanks rolled through the streets. There was a shortage of food. The insecurity about what would arise from this grew ever stronger. Then her best childhood friend died in Transnistria. Thirty years later, Ilona would still mark the date of his death every year. They killed him and strung him up. That was enough. She was ready to leave, and her parents were ready to let her go. As Ilona left for Germany, a part of her remained with her parents and in Moldova. Feelings of guilt have nagged at her ever since. But she dared not stay. She did not want her child to face such an uncertain future.

Her arrival in Germany in 1991 was hard. Ilona's family were able to immigrate on a legal basis as *Aussiedler* because of her husband's family history. They spent the first months in asylum-seeker housing; they learnt German and tried to understand what they had gotten themselves into. In Germany, no one needed a teacher of the Russian language. Her knowledge held no value there. Despite the recognition of her diploma, she would have had to study again. Later, maybe. At that time, it was more pressing that her husband could repeat his education in Germany in order to validate his previous education in the eyes of the German authorities. Ilona found herself in a situation with a husband in education, where she had to work, study and care for a child. All of this without a care structure, without friends or family to support them. Unthinkable. She worked wherever she found work. Settling in was a struggle anyway: a new language, informal work relations and discrimination. Sewing and cleaning in rich German households were her first jobs and threatened her dignity. She never told her parents what she was working as in Germany. At one point, she found formal employment in a hotel: room service, serving breakfast. After some years: a sales job. These were good steps. But then she fell ill. Ilona spent many months in various hospitals over the subsequent years while her husband was way out of his depth with emigration and life itself, incapable, unreliable and offensive.

She recovered, found a better sales job and, after several years, even worked her way up from sales assistant to branch manager. Her Russian language skills were helpful now, as many clients were tourists from Russia. But the money wasn't enough, not enough to survive as a single mother and support her family in Moldova. Her debts were mounting. Nevertheless, she got up every day, always stood her ground. She had always been a fighter. She learned how to walk proud. She never shared her pain. Why would she? There was no one to catch her anyway. This was her life experience from being in Germany. Twenty years she worked in sales. That shaped her. Literature and considering ethical questions – that was ancient history. There was no time for reading and philosophizing. That was the privilege of others. Still, having been a teacher in the past remained an important part of her self-understanding, a part that she had never completely given away. Then, a further step: a new job in an office.

Ilona built up a new life, worked, got out of debt, entered a new marriage, changed homes. Her life had changed constantly, was stressful and made her ill. She cared for her family in Moldova, worked, shouldered responsibilities. Her body went on strike; mandatory break. "Enough, I won't go on." She began talking about working in education again. What she had not dared to think for 25 years, she allowed it now. This change could happen because of the break that came with her illness; it could happen because she was out of debt, because of the social stability in her life, because of her better-paid office job that helped her gain confidence. Jobless, she began to dream: "I won't go back into sales." "Help me write applications," she asked her daughter. The two of them knew that it would be a tough endeavor. In a society of quantification and standards, life experience has no worth without corresponding diplomas. Add to this a deeply rooted xenophobia and racism; a Russian accent in Germany never facilitates a sense of togetherness. Ilona did not expect to find work as an educator, but she worked towards it. Desperation had never been her thing.

It was 2017 when she started searching for a new job. The situation in Germany had changed since her arrival in 1991. The accelerating destruction of the world through exploitation, poverty and war forced ever more people to flee the most ravaged regions. Hence, more and more people arrived in those countries profiting the most, such as Germany. Immediately, other people founded companies in order to profit financially from flight and persecution. For others, not least for those largely excluded from the labor market by their own history of migration, new work opportunities opened up in administration, infrastructure and social work. Ilona did not have to wait long. Soon she was invited for a job interview at a youth center for a position as a supervisor for unaccompanied minor asylum seekers. Her own story and the self-confidence, established over decades in Germany, were convincing. She got the job.

Finally, Ilona could work as an educator again, using her emotional intelligence first, instead of mainly serving others. She was suddenly involved again in reflecting on and answering ethical and pedagogical questions, and a world opened up that she had been excluded from for a long time. It made her happy and it made her father proud. She could challenge herself and discover new questions. Her own life trajectory, her own experiences of migration, of displacement and dispossession, of devaluation and discrimination, facilitated her access to the youngsters in a way that she felt her German co-workers often lacked. She knew what it felt like to arrive in a society that doesn't really welcome you, even if her life trajectory differed from these kids' experiences. She listened to stories of how the kids crossed the Mediterranean on a boat, what it means to see people drown. And while she listened to stories of death, mistreatment and trauma, she could connect with their feelings of being far away from family, of lacking a feeling of security. Ilona understood what pressure the young people coped with when they bore the responsibility of supporting families in their countries of origin. And they could exchange coping strategies: "Don't lose yourself in feeling responsible." This was a painful lesson Ilona had been learning over decades. It made her sad when the kids told her how people crossed the street whenever they saw them coming. These were experiences of racism she herself had never been confronted with. She worried when they could not find a landlord who would let a space to them. While back in Moldova, she had interpreted from literature to pupils. She now interpreted from the young people to her co-workers and the involved institutions, explained why the youngsters were sometimes angry or disappointed. Eventually, her responsibilities expanded: she had to supervise families with kids with special educational needs, no matter what their origin.

Once, Ilona accompanied a young woman of German origin to her psychologist's office. The young woman asked Ilona to remain present during the whole conversation. "I hide nothing from Ilona. I want her to stay," she said to her psychologist. Ilona stayed. She listened, explained and mediated. After the conversation, the therapist asked Ilona to stay back for a moment. "Could you support me at a meeting? It is a Russian family. I would like you to translate. You fill the gaps. Finish my sentences and thoughts. You think stuff through with me and help me. People might understand better when you talk to them. Can you do that?" she asked. "Of course, gladly," Ilona answered. Henceforth, the therapist asked for Ilona on a regular basis. She now interprets on many different levels, during her work and beyond. She translates languages and perspectives, experiences and feelings. She translates for those affected by inequalities and to those who have always been privileged.

Juldé

by Carlos Pestana

Between 1961 and 1974, Portugal was involved in an armed conflict in Guinea-Bissau, Angola and Mozambique, where different local freedom-fighters aimed to gain independence from Portugal. Ruled by a dictatorship since 1926, Portugal decided to send hundreds of thousands of soldiers from the European mainland to Africa in an effort to maintain its colonial empire. A defining characteristic of these wars was the deployment of numerous soldiers from a linguistically homogenous country, Portugal, to remote and linguistically diverse regions in Africa. One of the consequences was that the Portuguese army employed indigenous locals as embedded guides and translators. However, towards the end of the hostilities, more and more African soldiers were integrated into the regular army due to recruitment difficulties in Portugal. When, in 1974, the Carnation Revolution in Lisbon led to the end of this conflict, the number of Africans serving with Portuguese units in the three theatres exceeded the number of fighters from the independence groups.

Juldé was one such soldier serving in Guinea-Bissau in the early 1970s as a member of the Commandos, the elite troops of the Portuguese armed forces. He was born in colonial Guinea-Bissau, a multi-ethnic country in West Africa with a wide range of languages. He learned Portuguese at school. With his parents, he spoke Fula, but he also speaks Creole, the national language of Guinea. After completing the fourth grade, he started helping his father, a fisherman and farmer. At the age of 16, he was orphaned when his father was killed in an armed attack by the PAIGC, the most powerful group fighting for Guinea-Bissau's independence. He then decided to join the local self-defence militias. Armed and trained by the Portuguese, militias were supposed to protect villages from the PAIGC. At the age of 18, Juldé was recruited by the Portuguese army and was later accepted as a volunteer in the Commandos. 'In the Commandos, I hoped to acquire knowledge which would help me to protect my village, like, for example, recognising and destroying anti-personnel mines.' His company was a mirror image of Guinea-Bissau's ethnic and linguistic diversity, and the soldiers spoke all kinds of languages among themselves. Only with the commander did they speak Portuguese, since he did not speak any of the local languages. As an elite soldier, Juldé participated in operations in the wilderness that lasted up to several days. 'We often jumped out of helicopters and then headed towards our final goal. In those moments, it was kill or be killed.'

In such environments, the Portuguese army had encounters with people who did not speak Portuguese. If the commander on the ground was a white Portuguese, the use of translators was inevitable. In Juldé's company, it was the soldiers themselves who assumed this role, not only to try to assess the living conditions of isolated villages in the bush, but also to try to obtain information on enemy movements or to interrogate captured enemies. Juldé mentions that in these types of encounter, the first concern was ascertaining which language the intercepted person spoke and which soldier knew that language. This determined who would be the intermediary in the conversation between the commander on the ground and the person being interrogated. It was up to the commanding officer to ask the questions, while the mediating soldier translated them and later communicated to him the response of the person being questioned. Sometimes, Juldé's company found people in the jungle who were fleeing from areas where fighting had taken place. In these cases, they tried to convince the people to head to places under control of the Portuguese army. These were moments where one soldier served as a mediator between the Portuguese-speaking captain and the intercepted people, asking questions like: 'Why are you here?' Or explaining: 'We want to end the war so that you can go back to your villages. Don't stay in the jungle. In the jungle there are a lot of diseases. Come with us. We can bring you to the city.'

Because his company was proficient in the local languages, conversations during encounters could also take place quite spontaneously. However, at these moments, communication could face new types of obstacles. Juldé mentions a situation where his enemy interlocutor questioned Juldé's legitimacy to participate in that interaction on the grounds of military hierarchy: 'Once, we captured an officer of the PAIGC who spoke Creole like me. When I informed him that he should consider himself a prisoner of the Portuguese army, he replied "Who are you? You don't have the right to order my incarceration. I am an officer of the PAIGC and you are a simple soldier. Go and get your officer! He is the only one who has the right to say whether I am a prisoner or not."'

When asked about the peculiarities of situations of mediation, Juldé says that, far from belonging to the most relevant personal memories of the almost four years he fought for the Portuguese army in Guinea-Bissau, it was not an issue that made him reflect too much or made him feel very uncomfortable, being simply part of his daily tasks as a soldier. In fact, this function was never highly valued by his superiors and he was never decorated for these services. A decoration was given to him for bravery in combat, but not for mediation services. Juldé always tried to correctly translate any orders received, while treating with the utmost respect all those involved. He justifies this by saying that the attitude at the time was that in war, there is no revenge. Juldé insists that the Portuguese troops in Guinea-Bissau had express orders from the governor of Guinea-Bissau at the time, General Spínola, to treat well not only the population but also any captured enemy. Any fighters wounded in combat were to be evacuated, even those belonging to the enemy. When capturing an enemy, they would try to convince him to leave the bush and return to his village. Nevertheless, armed people were under no circumstances to be allowed to stay in the bush.

With the end of hostilities in 1974, a transition government led by the PAIGC took power in Guinea-Bissau. This government viewed men like Juldé with suspicion, not only because they had fought for the colonialist enemy, but also because they possessed military skills which could be dangerous to the new government. In fact, the early post-colonial era in the former Portuguese colonies was characterised by political instability in Guinea-Bissau and by civil wars in Angola and Mozambique.

Many of the men who were involved in these struggles had fought for the Portuguese army.

Juldé intended to stay in Guinea-Bissau and to contribute to the construction of a new country. According to him, there were negotiations between the Portuguese authorities and the PAIGC which persuaded many former members of the Portuguese army to surrender their weapons. This was after they learned of a letter – allegedly signed by the President of the Portuguese Republic, General Spínola, the respected former military chief of the Portuguese troops in Guinea-Bissau – telling them to lay down their arms. However, this put them at the mercy of the PAIGC, and many were consequently arrested or even shot. Juldé hesitated to leave the country despite these threats, but then a warning from a member of the PAIGC led Juldé to decide to flee to Senegal. There, after years of waiting and with the help of the Association of Portuguese Commandos, he obtained a Portuguese passport. He has since taken up residence in Portugal and transferred his family from Guinea-Bissau. In Portugal, Juldé worked for a long time as a security guard. He is now retired.

To my knowledge, there are no figures to show how many African men who fought for the Portuguese army, whether demobilised or regulars, were allowed to go to Portugal after the Carnation Revolution. In fact, very little is known about these men. Who were they? What was their motivation to fight for the Portuguese? What do their lives look like in Portugal? What is their relationship to the countries they came from? What did their language repertoire mean in their life? We should learn from these men while they are still alive to teach us.

Manu

by Sabine Lehner

I met Manu (not her real name) a couple of years ago when I conducted ethnographic research for my PhD project in a (now closed) basic care facility for asylum seekers in Austria. Manu worked there as a social worker. After the facility was shut down, she worked as a freelance interpreter. Although I only occasionally worked with her directly, I often happened to end up in her office, talking about the institution, current problems and all sorts of things. There, I was able to witness her and her colleague carefully listening to the residents and, whenever possible, taking care of their concerns and struggles in a structure that did not allow for much intervention.

Manu was born and raised in an Arabic-speaking country. After she obtained her high-school diploma, she wanted to study law, but did not have the right diploma to pursue her dream at the national universities. She therefore studied law in another Arabic-speaking country in the Middle East. Although she was initially afraid to move to, as she puts it, "the powder keg Middle East," she later considered it to be the most beautiful period of her life. During her stay there, she became familiar with other varieties of Arabic, which proved to be an important asset for her later work at the facility in Austria. After her graduation, Manu decided to move to Austria, owing to her father's enthusiasm for this country. She had her law certificate translated and notarized, but struggled with its formal validation in Austria. Since her degree was not fully recognized, she had to take some classes and restart studying law in German. Manu studied a lot and worked hard (though she eventually dropped out of her studies).

During her studies, she started to translate documents of all kinds for Arabic-speaking diplomats, from Arabic into English and vice versa. As she continually improved her German, she also began translating into this language. It wasn't just her linguistic competence that proved useful, but also her academic and profound legal knowledge in German and Arabic which enabled her to make precise translations of legal texts. Interestingly, it was not her first choice to become an interpreter. Rather, she describes it as "inevitable" that she was asked to interpret or to accompany friends and family. In fact, it was only later, when she already worked in various social projects with migrants and refugees, that her colleagues wondered why she was not registered as an interpreter, given that she possessed the "right" linguistic capital (Arabic) and was familiar with the field. Hence, they suggested that she should apply to get her name on the list of Arabic interpreters. Since then, Manu has worked as a translator and interpreter in various fields and institutions in Austria, in formal and informal settings, but only rarely as her main or full-time job. Overall, she does not consider herself a "typical interpreter" since she has not completed any formal training. She has acquired her translating and interpreting skills on her own.

As mentioned, Manu's work at the basic care facility for asylum seekers was primarily that of a social worker. Given her linguistic competences in Arabic, she often had to interpret for residents in various contexts, such as communicating with doctors, the police or during residents' meetings. She also assisted with phone calls with various local authorities and was asked by her colleagues to help and interpret for them. Therefore, she often had less time to concentrate on her main tasks, which included the organization of educational programs, future housing for the residents or support in all kinds of legal procedures. For these, Manu was again able to mobilize and capitalize on her legal knowledge.

Manu told me that some of the newly arrived residents in the facility initially were quite skeptical and cautious towards her. Although their shared Arabic and Muslim background immediately created the basis for trust, some residents only slowly and cautiously approached her to check, as she said with a laugh, "if this non-veiled little brown woman, who wears tight-fitting trousers and publicly smokes, is trustworthy." This surprised me, as I had never witnessed any overt suspicion or doubts on the part of the residents towards Manu, even if I once or twice observed residents taken by surprise when Manu answered in Arabic. To the contrary, she gained the trust of many residents, and children often, as she put it, "occupied" her office, enjoying her company, playing and talking with her. Manu told me that some residents hoped that she, as an Arabic speaker, would understand them and be able to solve their problems. Due to her previous work experience in interpreting, Manu was already used to these kinds of challenging expectations and was able to distance herself. For her, Arabic was a means of direct access to the residents, which helped her explain things more easily. In addition to Arabic, her English competences proved to be important for communicating with residents who did not speak Arabic. After a while, Manu tried to avoid relying on Arabic when communicating with the residents, since she was primarily a social worker and did not want her non-Arabic-speaking colleagues to be disadvantaged. Everyone had their own area of responsibility, and Manu did not want the Arabic-speaking residents to turn solely to her regarding every problem, especially when it concerned her colleagues' fields of expertise. Furthermore, she thereby tried to push the residents to speak German.

Since the facility was shut down, Manu has worked as a freelance interpreter for a municipal office for social affairs, interpreting for social workers and Arabic-speaking clients in often difficult and grave cases. She appreciates the cooperation with the social workers and is impressed by their professionalism. Although she likes the work, she describes her current job as challenging in many ways. One major challenge for her is that she is often torn between her professional ideology of being neutral and solely conveying what social workers and clients say on the one hand, and the clients' expectations of "loyalty" on the other. Although she works for the state, many clients expect her to be an ally, since they share the same language, as well as a seemingly similar cultural and religious background. Apparently, many clients, many of whom have only recently moved to Austria, are familiar with neither the interpreter's role nor the institution's task. Clients are often disappointed when Manu refuses to give them her phone number, which, as she explains, is highly unusual and rude in the eyes of Arabic-speaking people.

Instead, Manu refers them to the social workers in charge, in case they have any questions. Driven by such disappointment and misconception, some clients allegedly "punish" interpreters who refuse to cooperate in this way by complaining about the quality of the interpretation or claiming that they were not able to understand the interpreter's variety of Arabic. As a consequence, interpreters may be withdrawn from cases and replaced, losing money and risking damage to their reputation. In many cases, their successors realize that it was not due to bad quality, but due to "wrong" expectations as to the role of interpreters during the procedure. This is one reason why Manu wishes and argues for more cooperation and exchange among her colleagues – the other interpreters and social workers. Manu tries hard to distance herself, but still struggles with it since she considers herself not capable of cutting people off in this "inhuman" way, as some clients put it. Moreover, despite her efforts to be neutral, social workers occasionally ask Manu about her impression of the situation and the clients, given that she directly interacted with them.

Although she manages to deal with this mentally challenging work, she is aware of its risks and precarious conditions, such as an instable income or secondary traumatization. Generally, Manu is content with her current income, although it varies from month to month depending on how many cases she works on. However, she acknowledges that this might be problematic for some people. And, regardless of the emotional challenges, she enjoys the flexibility and the varied tasks. In Manu's view, interpreting is only a secondary job, in which she accompanies people for a specific purpose and only a limited amount of time, and then moves on.

Recently, Manu has observed two opposing trends in the field of interpreting in the social services sector in Austria, especially in the aftermath of 2015, when many displaced people (from Syria or other countries in the Middle East) came to Austria and there was a sudden need for interpreters. On the one hand, she notes that many multilingual people who possess a German certificate on a B1 or B2 level are assumed to be competent translators and interpreters, but apparently perform poorly. In the light of the sudden demand for Arabic-speaking people,

Manu was able to work in a social work team at that time. On the other hand, she identifies a trend of certification and professionalization, bringing a need for formal education in order to be employed as a social worker or interpreter in specific areas, such as asylum-seeker facilities. However, although Manu would probably, therefore, no longer qualify to work as a social worker and interpreter, she is not worried about her personal future, since she regards herself as having a good network. Being able to translate in Arabic, English and German makes her optimistic about the future.

Mme T, Janet, Ginny, Lyne, Masha, Anna, Paulette and Monica

by Monica Heller

It is the summer of 1974. I'm a university student, and I am lucky to have found a summer job; it will really help with all the costs of going to school. It is also a great job: I'm a clerk at the appointments desk of the outpatient department at a large hospital in downtown Montréal. From 8am to 4pm or 9am to 5pm, Monday through Friday. Essentially, I provide a body to replace my full-time co-workers as they each take their few weeks of summer holiday.

The Mohawk name for Montréal is Tiohtià:ke. I have seen this rendered as 'broken in two' or 'the place where groups separate'. This is linked to the fact that Montréal is the largest of a set of islands at the confluence of what are now called the Ottawa and Saint Lawrence Rivers, and was thus an indigenous meeting place for trade and for setting off on hunting and fishing expeditions. At the same time, these meanings have relevance for the struggle between French and English settler colonial populations into the present day. For the hospital, it means two things. One is that it belongs to the 'English' half of the dual French Catholic/English Protestant institutional duality, but it actually attracts staff and patients from all the ethnolinguistic and religious groups in the city (the reasons for this are too complex to entertain here). The second relevant aspect is that the hospital is situated just barely on the English side of the dividing line between 'French' and 'English' halves of the city, on the edge of the buffer zone where most immigrant groups start out.

The outpatient clinic is located through a hospital side door. Some people call in, but more come to the counter. It's a busy, noisy place. Our job is mainly talking, with some record-keeping – of appointments, of course. The people we talk to speak a lot of different languages: French and English of course, but also Italian, Portuguese, Greek, Hindi, Cantonese.

Behind the counter, we are all women. I'm the youngest; for everyone else, this is a full-time job, and considered a good one. It's stable and relatively well paid, although it belongs to the category of female service jobs in which not much upward mobility is possible. The ethos is definitely consistent with that of most female-gendered service occupations, intensified by the fact that this is a hospital and we are caring for patients. Our boss, Mme T, reminds us regularly that we must focus on helping the people who come to the hospital seeking care, and respect the doctors who devote their lives to providing it.

Mme T is a French Canadian married to a Bulgarian. She uses the short form because, she says, no one can pronounce her married name properly. She has been working at the hospital for over 20 years. Janet (who has been there about 10 years), and Ginny (who has been there almost as long as Mme T) speak English, though they understand a lot of French. Lyne, with about 15 years of service, is French Canadian. Her daughter has followed her into the hospital and works as a clerk in the records centre, where the medical files are kept. Masha and Anna, the newbies, are Czech and Italian, respectively. We share linguistic resources with the ladies from Registration next to us, especially with the one who speaks Greek (because none of us do), and sometimes with Paulette, a French Canadian who works in the emergency room down the hall (the line between emergency and outpatient isn't always clear). Everyone in this gang can speak English pretty well. French is the next most widely shared language. I can also get by in Spanish, but, in 1974, there isn't much need for it.

One afternoon, Janet is on phone duty, usually reserved for those with seniority: Janet, Ginny and Lyne. You get to have one conversation at a time, and people can't stare at you angrily for not being able to get them an appointment when they want it. 'Monica!' she calls out, 'Come over here. I can't understand this.

It's in French.' I take the phone; Janet sits beside me. The voice on the other end of the line is speaking rapidly, sounding distressed. It turns out the man has tried to cut off his penis. Really, he should be in an ambulance, and this situation is way beyond anything I have yet encountered. We call over Mme T; she speaks on the phone while Janet and I confer about the nature of the situation and whether it is faster to run over to Paulette in ER down the hall or to try to call her; probably the first, since the person on the phone called us precisely because contact with ER was impossible. Between us, Mme T, Paulette, Janet and I arrive at a shared understanding of what is going on and what to do about it.

Later, Anna is trying to help Masha with an Italian patient and Lyne is on the line with a doctor who is most comfortable in English, but who is trying to get help from Lyne with a French-speaking patient. As far as I can make out, they are all speaking French and English in an effort to get things straight: what the doctor wants, what the appointments desk can provide, what works for the patient. I speak English to a patient whose hospital card says 'Murphy', but who only speaks French, and French to one named 'Larivière', but who only speaks English. I have to explain something about what will happen at the orthopaedic clinic to Mme Murphy, but the doctor's note is in English, and in any case, I am not sure what it means in any language. I ask Lyne, who is sitting next to me. She doesn't know. 'Ask Mme T', she says. Mme T isn't sure either, but she knows what the procedure is, at least, and so we settle on something that seems understandable, even if that isn't what a medical manual would call it. We write the English term down so, when things get calmer, we can ask around and find out how to say it properly in French.

Getting socialised into this collective practice will serve me well all my life, albeit perhaps more for writing than for talking. Writing memos, research grants, press releases and academic articles have all required tacking back, forth and through at least French and English, and often other languages as well. All have involved intensive collaboration between all kinds of people, mostly across different positions in the workplace (it is common to find a professor or two, a student, a project coordinator and an administrative assistant gathered in the entrance space of a university department debating terminology, formulations and textual interpretation); but sometimes also extending out to friends and family members (texting has facilitated the extension of the collective interpretation network immeasurably). Women, though, are often at the centre of such collectives. If you want to know what the best translation/interpretation internet site is, ask your administrative assistant.

Narendra

by Sebastian Muth

Narendra is always on call, as a medical interpreter and translator of medical records and invoices, as a coordinator of patient
appointments, as a tourist guide in between hospital visits, and
as a Russian-speaking point of reference for medical tourists
in a foreign country. Narendra is called a "marketing specialist" by Centurion Hospital, his employer on the outskirts of
India's capital, Delhi. However, most of the time, it is his job to
interpret for Russian-speaking medical tourists from countries
of the former Soviet Union. He has been in professional employment as a language worker for almost a decade and looks back at
a career as an accountant and back-office operator working for
multinational corporations in and around Delhi. In that respect,
service work in languages other than his native Hindi has always
been part of his professional trajectory since he completed his
MA in Russian at the prestigious Delhi University in 2010. He
began studying Russian in 2007 with a certificate course equiva-
lent to a BA, but at that time his motivation for the subject was
largely based on family advice rather than, as he recalls, any
informed knowledge of the opportunities proficiency in Russian
might bring for employment anywhere, let alone in the private
medical sector. In fact, it was his nephew, a liaison officer in the
Indian Navy at the time, who convinced him to build a career
on Russian, as, in his own words, "India and the Soviet Union
always had close ties." While this historicizing discourse on the
value of Russian was prominent among some of his classmates
at the university, Narendra had little knowledge of Russia and
the post-Soviet sphere. He got in touch with first-language
Russian-speakers only when teachers started to broker him as an
interpreter and guide for tour groups from Russia.

These tour-guiding jobs could not fully sustain him, but did help him to get by as a student and, more importantly, convinced him that a career based on his Russian skills was possible. Once, when we talked about the reasons he ended up in medical tourism, Narendra was able to put this conviction down to a single key moment when, after guiding Russian tourists through the sites of historic Delhi, he received a 100-dollar tip on top of what was negotiated as pay. He admitted that being able to see his efforts in learning Russian pay off in the form of an American banknote that matched his monthly budget as a student in Delhi was stunning. Further, it convinced him that, as long as he tried his best, rewards would follow. Of course, things didn't always go precisely this way, but he nevertheless continued to work for tour groups up until his graduation. During that time, he learned that tour guiding also pays off in a number of other ways. Apart from personal monetary gain, the Russian language service has added value and assured the attractiveness of his product for the last decade. Over time, he learned that there are specific places and activities which Russian-speakers appreciate in and around Delhi, particularly certain markets, shops and shopping malls. Consequently, putting these on his itineraries paid off in yet another way: he was able to strike deals with shop-owners, steering his tourists towards shops offering products they would likely appreciate (such as leather goods or furs), with Narendra getting a commission on each purchase his Russian guests made.

After graduation, he sought more stable and predictable employment, and his Russian skills secured him just that. He became an accountant in one of the numerous business-out-sourcing hubs that sprang up in and around Delhi in the early 2000s, writing invoices in Russian for companies in Russia, a job that, as he recalls, made him forget most of his conversational knowledge of the language. This and other jobs meant stability for him and ensured a certain level of prestige among his family and friends. He worked regular hours in air-conditioned offices and, while it was modest, he appreciated the stable income he could always count on. However, he continued to stay in touch with his fellow alumni from Delhi University, hoping for new opportunities and ways to reconnect to those days of tour-guiding when, for him, dedication and initiative could make everything

possible. This moment arrived when he saw a post in a Facebook
group of current and former students and current learners of
Russian in the Delhi area; the key Russian speaker at Centurion,
a large private hospital in Delhi owned by one of India's in-
dustrial conglomerates, had just left his position. There was not
even a formal job posting, but as soon as he saw the message, he
rang human resources at Centurion and, a day later, became a
marketing specialist, patient manager, and medical interpreter
for international guests, in his case patients who prefer to (or
can only) interact in Russian. As he already had experience in interpreting and fondly remembered his encounters with Russian
tourists (and their generosity), working at the "International
Lounge" was clearly a step up from what he had been doing
before. As in his earlier days of tour-guiding, his Russian skills
meant an added value, but this time not only for him, but for
the hospital as well. What was appealing was the prospect of
working with "real people" in an international environment, and
while his gross monthly income of 19,000 rupees (roughly 250
US dollars) is about 20 percent below the average income in the
Indian capital, Narendra is not worse off than before. Also, for
the first time in his career, he is managing others, as he oversees
three recent graduates in Russian, whose employment is decided
on a month-by-month basis to help Narendra when there are
more Russian-speaking patients than he can handle by himself.

The people he cares for do not conform to the image that
medical tourism is all about entitlement and informed choice,
but instead are emblematic of global health inequalities and
the lack of access to proper healthcare in their home countries.
Narendra's patients primarily come from all over the post-Soviet
sphere, particularly from Tajikistan, Turkmenistan, Uzbekistan,
and Kazakhstan. Most of them arrive with liver problems, need
spinal surgery, have diabetes or kidney problems, seek oncological
treatment, or simply require medical check-ups. During his work
hours, he literally seems to be running around the hospital,
rushing from one patient to another to communicate with doctors
about treatment plans, to interpret doctor–patient interactions,
to prepare the patients' paperwork and explain procedures,
and to retrieve invoices and explain these to patients. Also, Narendra
organizes transfers for incoming/outgoing patients, takes care of

their accommodation, and organizes the shifts of his subordinate interpreters. Work for these interpreters and patient managers is organized in four shifts: the most junior interpreter gets the night shift, then there's an early morning shift, the day shift (Narendra usually assigns himself that one), and a late evening shift. In addition, the three interpreters on monthly contracts take turns for what Narendra calls the "rotational airport shift," which involves greeting patients at Indira Gandhi Airport with a bilingual English and Russian placard bearing the patient's name and Centurion's logo. During this shift (for which there is no extra pay), the interpreters also take care that the patients and their relatives reach their pre-booked accommodation, typically located opposite the hospital, in guesthouses that have contracts with Centurion.

Narendra must also make sure that at least one interpreter is always physically present at the hospital. For his work, his mobile phone is his main work tool, used to communicate with patients (he organizes sim cards for them or they chat via WhatsApp), as well as doctors and co-interpreters, to access his Russian online dictionary, and to look up English medical terms he does not know. Narendra is confident about his Russian and rarely runs into problems. However, he has trouble when doctors speak in English and not Hindi, and he finds it extremely difficult to interpret from English into Russian. Even more problematically, for the doctors, English alone seems to be the indicator of his value as a professional. Ironically though, regardless of what they think of him, doctors nevertheless rely on Narendra as someone who can explain medical procedures they do not wish to bother going into detail about (like how a liver transplant works, how a vasectomy is performed, or what happens during an endoscopic procedure). At times, the job is strenuous, yet Narendra cannot let this show. While his work hours are predictable, any emotional stress attached to caring for his patients isn't. Obviously, treatment sometimes fails and, at times, patients are sent home terminally ill and penniless. Narendra laments this, but can do nothing about it, both because of his subordinate position within the hospital, and because he has become an integral part of his employer's internationalization efforts. What he can do, however, is subvert the system and become an advocate for patients, rather than the private hospital. He does so through small interventions: recommending external (and cheaper) diagnostics services, organizing cut-price accommodation for the families of his patients, or buying medication for those patients who leave Centurion for their Central Asian homes healthy but broke. For him, these moments of showing empathy when no one else does are what make him carry on with the job.

Nima

by Nima Jebelli and Sibo Kanobana

Nima and I have been friends for nearly 15 years. We both have a keen interest in languages and when we met, we both worked in the same sector: I as a language teacher for migrants and he as an interpreter, also for migrants. As people of color who were raised in a predominantly white environment, we discovered that we asked the same questions about the world and our place in it. We established our friendship around long and serious conversations about race, gender, sexuality, politics, and ethics. Surprisingly, we rarely linked these talks with what we did at work. So when I started to do research and was asked to write a portrait of an interpreter, I thought about Nima. Somehow, I knew that Nima's story would also be my story, even if I had never worked as an interpreter and even if they had rarely told me anything about their job.

I interviewed them for more than two hours, made a transcript, and reworked it into a six-page story. I wasn't satisfied. The conversation had triggered new questions. I sent them the story anyway and asked them to review it. After some rewriting and discussion, they decided to start over from scratch. They delivered a text I loved and, after some minor changes and editing, we agreed upon the text you can read below.

Ever since I was a child, I have been explaining to people why I am not white. Why my name is not Bart or Peter. What this strange other language is that I speak. Where I am *really* from and whether or not I go back there sometimes.

For as long as I can remember, I have been white people's object of study. A curiosity. So when a friend in academia wanted to do a piece on interpreting, based on my experience as a public service interpreter, I wasn't surprised. I was surprised, though, to hear that it did not have to be anything prosaic or academic. *Some literary freedom is permitted*, he said.

Alright then.

When I was seven, a Catholic priest asked my parents if he could *borrow me* for his Bible class. The next Sunday, I was introduced to a group of Muslim kids my age as *Nima, the Muslim boy from Iran*, and was kindly asked to show the other kids how we talk, eat, and pray. I had never prayed before. I had never seen my *atheist* parents pray. But I had seen some relatives do it in Iran. So I gave the Belgian priest and his Bible boys one hell of a performance that Sunday morning in 1988, bending and standing and kneeling at random in all earnestness with my eyes shut.

Since then, I have been providing the white world, my white world, with what they want: the image of an outstanding immigrant. I have mastered this skill of putting people at ease about Foreignness, Race, Immigration, and Islam. Happy to oblige.

In general, any job is good enough for the immigrant. The immigrant cannot afford to be unemployed. But what about the Good Immigrant? No profession suits them better than interpreting.

The social function of the Good Immigrant turned Interpreter is twofold. On the one hand, I show the new arrivals from Iran or Afghanistan what great prospects they have if they adapt and assimilate and learn the language: "Chances are very slim you'll ever become a therapist or a medical doctor, but you *might* become an interpreter. If you work hard enough."

On the other hand, I'm constantly proving to white healthcare or welfare professionals what a useful immigrant I am. Only as an interpreter – enabling the white professional to work with immigrants – is my presence as a person of color legitimate. I need to hang on to this for dear life. My white colleagues don't have to legitimize their presence. (Do white people ever have to legitimize their presence?) I have actually earned my place in white society. Kudos for that. Kudos to me. Everyone's happy.

Now you may think that I sound angry. And guess what: I am.

I am tired.

I'm tired of performing. I am tired of bending over to make a bridge out of my back. I am tired of smiling and being nice and proving to you – you, the white privileged citizen – that I am one of the good ones. "You, Nima, are definitely a good one. It's those others that give you a bad name."

I am tired of interpreting. My back is aching. Build your own bridge! Go look elsewhere for that smile, those white teeth, that Good Immigrant!

Many stories have I heard, of young and old, Iranians and Afghans alike, raped and beaten and abused. I voiced their words, translated their expressions. But I could never help or comfort them. I brought them no solace. Luckily for me, the interpreter's code of conduct forbids this anyway: never take sides, never get involved, never correct, assist or help anyone. Just stick to the words spoken. Translate what you hear and stay out of the conversation.

My first interpreting job was for a middle-aged Iranian man. I came fresh out of the community interpreting course. Against protocol, I joined the patient in the waiting room prior to his doctor's appointment. Even more against protocol, I gave the man my phone number when he asked for it. While he was writing it on a piece of paper, I thought, well, this is exactly what I was taught *not* to do.

This man was so desperate about his wife having left him and taken the kids with her that he took his own life before our second appointment. I remember thinking: good thing he didn't call me. What would I have done?

After that, I never gave anyone my phone number or any other information again. I never slipped.

The good interpreter shows no mercy. They are a lone wolf. Makes no friends. Keeps performing. They do not get involved and takes no sides. Just repeats the sender's code in the target code so the receiver may respond in their code. And vice versa. *Ad nauseam.*

Often, the newcomer is happy to be provided with an interpreter. Often, they are not.

Sometimes, the newcomer is happy with the professional distance the interpreter upholds. Sometimes, they are not.

Most people who arrive here from Iran and Afghanistan have never worked with a professional interpreter before. Their first reaction is a mix of relief and joy, to see a "fellow Iranian" beside them in the ordeals they have to go through as a patient or client of Dutch-speaking professionals in Belgium.

Their optimism, however, soon yields to disappointment – and sometimes even frustration – when they realize the interpreter is not exactly *on their side*.

Is this still a good interpreter? Are they a fellow Iranian? What are they? Where are they really from?

Unfortunately, I cannot help them answer that question. Yes, sure, I can tell them I am the interpreter and explain to them how the protocol works. This unyielding protocol. They will understand the words I am uttering. They know what *interpreter* and *neutral* and *confidential* mean. They know the words. But do they grasp the concept, and, more importantly, do they appreciate these terms?

They are given no choice other than to abide by the rules that the interpreting service – and, by extension, I – force upon them. They cannot say: "Please, help me out here. I am alone in this foreign land and need your friendship and guidance, and not just your strictly protocolled interpreting skills."

Well, no, technically they can. Sometimes they do. The good interpreter then converts the code and leaves it to the social worker, healthcare professional, or school teacher to handle the matter. Easy.

Ever since I was a child, I have been interpreting, been building bridges. Not because I wanted to, but because I had to. And you know what? I have been good at it. Obey the rules, enforce them, stick to protocol. Keep your distance.

As a good interpreter, I am only loyal to language. Language and protocol.

This is how I have earned my stripes. My tired stripes.

Non

by Priscilla Angela T. Cruz

Non is a woman in her sixties who is a whirlwind of creative energy. She is a Japanese woman living in the Philippines who, aside from being an interpreter, is a restaurateur, a chocolate maker, an advocate for zero-waste living, and an avid cyclist who uses her bike as her primary means of transport. It is a delight to be with her and listen as she talks about her many plans, such as establishing a zero-waste store, launching her own brand of ice cream, working with organic farmers, teaching origami, and hosting Japanese language classes.

She stumbled into interpreting after she retired. Originally, she was a veterinarian in Japan. She says she loved biology but was warned by her brother that if she studied biology, she would wind up a high school teacher, which felt so dead-end. So, she decided to be a vet. She mentions that her great-great-grand-father, a samurai, was given a ranch at the end of the Meiji Era in Japan for his services to the shogun. From that ranch came a dairy farm, that led to several generations of her family working with animals. As a vet, she worked for a dairy farmers' union; predictably, she took care of cows.

Her husband's job brought her to the US, where her children were raised American with English as their first language. During her many years in the US, she studied various fields to keep productive, like mechanical engineering, some medicine, and even journalism. As a journalism student, she mentions how she got an A+ on an exposé on textbooks, but quit her studies because of a very racist teacher who had all foreign students kicked out. Later on, after her husband had died and her kids had decided to settle in the States, she moved back to Japan as a woman of retirement age.

It's not surprising that retirement didn't suit Non, considering she describes herself as someone who always needs to be doing something. She says boredom is devastating, so she absolutely refused to live what she calls "the party lifestyle" – involving lunches out and small talk – of Japanese women in their fifties. So, on the advice of Filipino friends, at age 55, she packed her bags, bought an apartment in Quezon City, and moved to the Philippines in search of things to do. Her first job, at a Japanese travel agency, led her to interpreting.

She interprets for a wide variety of clients. She works with Japanese multinational companies, general managers, and sales managers who have business interests in the consumer-driven Philippine market. She also does what she calls "travel-related interpreting," which means she sits in booths at travel expos as, in her own words, "the token Japanese," to interpret materials and talk to prospective clients about Japan's prefectures. Furthermore, she works with labor companies who need her to interpret during job interviews involving Filipino engineers, salespeople, nurses, and caregivers who seek the greener pastures of Japan for work. She didn't apply to any firm to be an interpreter. She says she originally began the job as a "dustbin for emergency cases," someone who was called upon to take the place of an interpreter who was sick. Over the years, though, she eventually managed to get her own clients.

Despite her years of experience in interpreting, Non says she doesn't actually like the job. For one thing, she says that it's hard to find the right words. Because interpreting is meant to happen quickly, she doesn't have the time to make careful choices, and if she makes a mistake, she feels regret. Furthermore, she finds that being an interpreter relegates her to an "in-between" position. She explains that interpreting can require a lot of memorization, depending on the client. For example, if she interprets for businesspeople, she needs to memorize words related to the business. For general managers who are interested in contracts, for example, she needs to memorize the legalese in at least two languages. This takes a lot of time, but when she meets the clients, she finds that her task involves only receiving information in one language and recovering the words for that information in the other language. As she says, "something exists already, just remember it." She specifically describes this process as being unproductive because it "doesn't create anything."

Another reason she finds interpreting hard is that there are certain concepts which cannot easily be transferred into another language. For example, technical knowledge is very challenging to interpret, especially when she doesn't know the field. For this reason, she refuses to work for clients in politics or economics, because she knows she doesn't know enough about either field to be accurate. Cultural differences also involve difficult concepts to interpret. For example, in the Philippines, many families employ maids, which is very unusual in Japan. So, interpreting in a context where she has to talk about maids requires a lot of sensitivity as she not only needs the words but needs to also "interpret" the cultural and economic differences between Japan and the Philippines. She says that "interpreting is in the brain, but creating the voice is hard."

Instead of interpreting, Non prefers translating. She finds that translating affords her the opportunity to do research and, consequently, generate new knowledge. Translating is also a slower process than interpreting, so she gets to take her time, as she says, "understanding it in myself." Because she enjoys research, when she translates, she feels like she is digging for information, as well as producing and sharing knowledge. Recently, she joined a project that involved translating texts on the history of Christianity in Nagasaki and the Philippines, and the connection between the two places. She said she had to do a lot of research, some of which taught her how the *kanji* (Japanese characters) for certain words and concepts had changed over time. This type of work, because it creates something new, is something she considers valuable.

I first met Non a few years ago at her restaurant, Zaan Japanese Teahouse. When she was working with the travel agency, her boss brought her a sample of chocolate-covered mangoes. She tried it and exclaimed in Filipino, "hindi masarap" ("not delicious") and thought she could improve on the product. And so her own brand of chocolate, Tsoko-fino, was born. She makes all her chocolate by hand, using Philippine cacao, mangoes, and pili nuts. She opened Zaan because she needed a place to make her chocolates, which are now popular among Filipinos and Japanese alike.

Since I met her, Non has become a dear friend. I often meet her in Zaan, which is, as she intended, a slice of Japan in Quezon City. She has a *tatami* floor set-up and some plain wooden tables and chairs. She serves the food that the ordinary Japanese family eats everyday: *nabe* (hotpot), *okonomiyaki* (savory pancakes), *bonito and cheese raizu* (a small rice sandwich with dried seaweed), and desserts like *warabimochi* (little sweets made with rice flour and served with roasted soybean powder). Non has many plans for Zaan, like new food items, such as soy-based feta cheese and Japanese-style fruit-and-cream sandwiches. Zaan is also the venue for different cultural events like cooking classes and music nights involving traditional Japanese instruments. She is comfortably translingual, so she shuttles between Japanese, English, and Filipino when she talks to anyone who comes into her restaurant.

Considering how much she is occupied by the many projects that she loves, I ask why she persists in interpreting when she isn't so fond of the job. She responds by saying that it gives her three benefits. First, she invests her earnings in her restaurant. Through her interpreting money, she has additional cash to cover staff salaries, in case earnings are low, and to spend on new projects for Zaan. As she has a pension, she has enough to live very comfortably, but interpreting is a way for her to do more of what she wants to do. Thanks to interpreting, she gets extra cash for her passion projects. Second, she likes connecting with people, which interpreting allows her to do. She points out that "we are all *Homo sapiens* first before we are Japanese, Filipino, or any other nationality." It is this philosophy that leads her to welcome connections with everyone she meets.

Finally, she interprets because it relates to what she considers to be her life's work, and this is to represent what she calls "the real Japan." She explains this by talking about Japanese restaurants which go overboard with what they consider to be Japanese décor, so much that they end up being totally un-Japanese. So, she keeps the décor of Zaan simple, with almost bare walls save for a single scroll and a few shelves which hold her teaware. She says she agreed to do the project on Japanese Christians because these men and women were humble and disciplined, which is what the Japanese are. Doing this book project allowed her to represent the qualities of her people.

So, although Non dislikes interpreting, it is a job that she will hang on to while she is able. In a global capitalist age where it is so easy to equate the value of individuals to how much money they earn, Non teaches us a valuable lesson: find something tolerable to earn the money so you can do your life's work.

This piece was written before the Covid-19 pandemic. During the quarantine, Non closed her restaurant.

Peter

by Mi-Cha Flubacher

After his medical studies, my father opened his first practice as a general practitioner in 1982. As a young idealist of socialist conviction, he had decided to set up shop in one of the traditional working-class neighbourhoods of his hometown of Basel, Switzerland. As a result of Switzerland's labour policies and its practice of recruiting migrant workers in poorer regions from the 1950s onwards, the population of this neighbourhood was largely of Italian origin. As he spoke some Italian, he felt equipped to consult and treat Italian-speaking patients who did not have fluent command of German. In retrospect, he concludes that even if there were some misunderstandings and he did not always feel entirely linguistically secure, the communication with his patients generally worked out.

This situation changed quickly after the 1980 *coup d'état* in Turkey, which resulted in a severe crackdown in that country on leftists and trade unionists. Politically active people fled Turkey *en masse*. Some of them arrived in Basel, leading to a transformation of the linguistic makeup in this neighbourhood. Many of the political refugees coming to my father's practice were traumatised (for example by their imprisonment and/or torture), complicating the medical challenges and symptoms. Soon, he realised that the practice of *ad hoc* interpretation to which he had to resort with these new patients was not sufficient, as he simply could not get through to them. There was thus a growing awareness on his part that patients of other linguistic backgrounds experienced an automatic discrimination. This awareness was rendered even more acute by experiences from his private life. On the one hand, he witnessed the experiences of his wife, my mother, who was originally from Korea and did not speak German when she arrived in Switzerland as a trained nurse. On the other hand, he himself had experienced situations in Korea where he had no chance of following a conversation without knowledge of Korean and was dependent on his wife for interpreting. In sum, these experiences and observations led to a fundamental desire to understand his patients and to be understood by them, which drove him to look for solutions.

As my father told me, he started looking for answers more systematically in the late 1980s: how to optimise multilingual and intercultural consultations. Most importantly, he joined several working groups consisting mostly of social workers and psychotherapists – though unfortunately few other GPs – in which issues concerning the migrant population in Basel were discussed from an interdisciplinary perspective. Aside from this practice-driven exchange, he also started reading into anthropological and psychiatric theories on the interplay of culture with health and illness. He learned that the patient-centric perspective, which privileges a good doctor–patient relationship, may actually ignore many other important personal relationships and sociological factors impacting on health and healing. In accordance with the epistemologies of the time, the aim was to develop an understanding of patients from other sociocultural backgrounds in a medical theoretical framework. Unfortunately, in my father's view, a lot of work since then has overemphasised 'culture' and 'cultural differences', while disregarding political and social dimensions. Such 'culturalisation', the stereotypical reduction of behaviour, communication etc., is a phenomenon he witnessed time and again in the treatment of migrant patients. Admittedly, no one is ever safe from making culturalist explanations or assumptions....

On a more concrete level, my father started working with a Turkish interpreter. Having arrived in Basel in the early 1980s as a political refugee from Turkey, she was working as an interpreter without any official certification and would come in every Saturday morning. In terms of payment, he adopted the fixed hourly rate used by HEKS, an aid organisation of the Swiss Protestant churches which had established the Turkish–German interpretation service Linguadukt at a hospital in Basel in 1987, as well as offering interpreter training and classes for specific (medical) vocabulary. Yet, the health insurance did not pay for interpretation or any other linguistic service, and working as a GP in his own practice, he did not have an institution such as the hospital to cover the costs incurred. In the end, he found a way to bill the interpretation as professional expenses.

Working with an interpreter, my father soon realised that something was going on not only on a communicative level but also on a personal level in his relations with patients. As word of mouth spread, many of his Turkish patients would simply drop in on Saturdays, because they knew that the interpreter would be there. Speaking in their own language, they could use their own voice in their own time. Some patients who had appeared passive at first contact suddenly opened up and became quite active when they got the chance to communicate in their own language. In the long run, he found that his observations confirmed assumptions made in medical literature on the empowerment of patients through interpretation. Working with an interpreter resulted in a change of rhythm as, quite naturally, a consultation with an interpreter required more time, but it also led to a change of control and power: all of a sudden, it was not the doctor who was in charge but the interpreter. After all, they were now in charge of the two linguistic repertoires, making the other interactants (doctor and patient) dependent on their mediation and needing to invest their trust in it. The dominant position automatically inhabited by the doctor in any doctor–patient interaction diminished a little bit, as the focus shifted onto the interpreter and their mediating role. Looking back, my father concludes that it is this potential loss of control and power over the interaction and its content (in addition to the loss of time) that deters many doctors from working with interpreters to this day. Ironically, my father argues, the initial time spent establishing a good mutual understanding would save time and money in the long run.

When the collaboration with his first interpreter ended after a few years, he found a replacement soon afterwards and continued working with interpreters until his retirement in the 2010s. The second Turkish interpreter he worked with was highly professional. In his view, they represented a team, discussing cases before and after consultation. It was of great help to him that he could tell her in advance what he aimed for in a consultation, because she then knew where to put emphasis or how to manage the interaction, and could also give him feedback. After she left, he worked with a string of other Turkish–German interpreters, whose quality differed greatly, and with whom he worked for varying lengths of time. Some failed to show up for appointments, while others were highly professional. Naturally, the personal relationship with him or his staff could also have played a part in the performance of the individual interpreter. Rarely did he work with interpreters of languages other than Turkish, but made use of his working knowledge of Italian, French and English whenever possible. When, at the turn of the millennium, the neighbourhood underwent another major transformation due to the war in what was then Yugoslavia, a third partner joined the clinic and took charge of the new patient groups and their linguistic profiles, finding his own communicative solutions.

To close on a personal note, my father insists that working with interpreters and, thus, engaging with patients on a deeper level, helped him battle an onset of cynicism, resulting from frustration and being overwhelmed by patients with exalted expectations of what he could do for them – beyond medical competences. Working with interpreters was thus just as valuable for him as for his patients. The interpreters apparently appreciated this work experience as well, with its regular schedule and institutionalised rate, without the racist and dismissive doctoral behaviour experienced elsewhere.

Pia

by Kamilla Kraft

Pia was the kind of interpreter who mediated all kinds of knowledge, impressions and feelings between people, whether they shared languages or not. Not only did she use her language proficiencies and communication competences to manage multilingual encounters on the transnational construction site where she worked, she also used them to mediate the social lives of workers and managers – an affective interpretation of sorts. In meetings and conversations with the rest of the management team, she would always be the one to provide a supportive smile when someone made a joke (even if it was not funny) or a chuckle to soften the tension of an awkward situation. At first, I tended to think of her laughter as an expression of uncertainty or even discomfort, until a colleague pointed out to me that 'Pia is the buddy of the team; she offers support all the time'. To this, I would add that she often also offered comfort and engaged in a great deal of care work. She would always lend an ear to complaints and stories of hardship. At some point, a couch was placed in the reception area where she had her desk. Soon, people started joking that they could come sit on the couch and get therapy sessions from her – and many ended up doing just that. Apart from comfort, she also provided moral discipline. When foremen and project leaders, her male colleagues, transgressed the rules of social politeness, such as by leaving someone who had booked a meeting with them to wait too long, she would interfere, politely reminding them of what time it was or that someone was waiting to see them. 'It is all about decency and respect for others' time', she confided to me when we were alone. Her domain was the reception; a place where everybody went – for help, information or coffee (always freshly brewed by Pia) – but also a place everybody passed through – like passengers in the halls of a railway station, barely noticing the surroundings on their way to somewhere else. I guess, this mirrored the most striking feature of Pia's linguistic, emotional and moral interpretation work – always central but rarely visible or audible. This also meant that her efforts were rarely noticed or recognised.

I met Pia on a construction site in Oslo. She was the project secretary, part of the management team and one of the few women in the workplace. In many ways, her interpretation work revolved closely around her job and her gender. The day we met was the first day on site for both of us. In fact, for Pia, it was her very first time on a construction site altogether.

In Norway, as in most places, construction sites are transnational stages where people with different cultural and linguistic backgrounds collaborate. Hence, communication is always a much discussed issue in these workplaces. However, there seems to be a common consensus that it is the foremen who are most affected by this feature of modern construction sites. After spending half a year with Pia, I would argue that a secretary does her fair share of interpretation and communication as well, though this, in contrast to the foreman's work, is often muted.

A construction site is also hierarchical, and so is the management team. Members are divided into administration, project planning and production, with a project leader on top. Production is the most prestigious area, with 'proper' construction work at its core, while administration has the lowest status. The contractor behind the management team hired all secretaries on a temporary basis before potentially offering them a permanent contract. This was to ensure that the secretaries 'worked out'. Pia had been hired through a major staffing agency on a 10-month contract. Prior to this job, she had worked on two short-term contracts. She told me that it would be nice to have a permanent job and some stability. But it was also exciting to get new experiences and colleagues all the time.

Pia tried as best she could to communicate with all her new colleagues. Apart from Norwegian, she spoke English and German, languages that she had studied throughout primary and secondary school and actively used in previous jobs. One of her primary tasks in this new job was to register the workers on the site and make sure they had been informed about safety regulations. These workers came from a range of different national and linguistic backgrounds: Polish, Norwegian, English, Russian, Swedish and more. Pia would show them a 13-minute video that was designed by the safety and security officer to *show* – without speech – safety information and regulations. Subsequently, the workers would have to sign a registration form, agreeing to the rules and confirming that they had understood them. While the video required no explanation on the part of Pia, it was a different matter with the registration forms, which were available in Norwegian only. In these moments of explanation, which occurred several times a week, a chain of interpretation would take place if the worker did not speak Norwegian. Pia would translate the form into English, explaining what it stated, what fields the new workers would have to fill in and what documentation she would need from them. If the workers did not understand English, Pia's explanations were in turn translated into a language they did understand by another worker or boss who knew English too. Seemingly, Pia and the workers always managed to arrive at some mutual understanding despite this cumbersome communication. Or at least the right forms were signed and the documentation acquired.

She also had to make weekly inspection rounds to check the workers' ID cards. During these rounds, there would not always be someone around who could interpret, but she still managed to convey to all workers that she needed to see their cards. Pointing and using simple words or expressions – yes, no, *njet*, *dobra*, ID, *okej*, *kaputt* – are often portrayed as a construction site register in and of itself, and before long Pia became fluent in it. Otherwise, she relied on English and Norwegian and rarely seemed uncertain about which language to choose. At times, she would even continue speaking English to an interlocutor who had already made it clear that he spoke Norwegian as well. Clearly, there was strong categorisation work at play in these encounters. One day, I mistook one of the Norwegian workers for one of the Poles, and I told Pia how I was always impressed by how effortlessly he seemed to switch between Norwegian and Polish. She replied: 'Oh no, he's Norwegian. But it's true. He looks like a Pole.' This moment exemplified how our identities are embodied and how actively others use them as semiotic resources for interpretation and meaning-making – resources that may become entwined with discrimination. It was also an illustration of how much we rely on such resources to socially navigate professional spaces, a reminder that practices which reproduce social stigma and inequality do not necessarily stem from ill-will, but from naturalised action and reasoning carried out in encounters, for example in an effort to do one's job.

Pia was not instructed in how to go about interactions with the workers on site, a challenge also faced by many foremen, who would often complain about the challenges they faced in their efforts to ensure communication with 'foreign' workers. She *was* instructed on how to perform another central task, namely creating and translating written texts. Her annoyance with the Norwegian-only registration forms meant that she wanted to translate as many of the written materials as possible. Yet, at least one of the foremen told her to use only Norwegian, an instruction that could be said not to comply with legislation. Apparently, it also ran counter to Pia's standards. While she overtly agreed to make Norwegian versions only, in practice she always made Norwegian and English versions. Most written texts she also wanted to translate into German, despite questions from the safety representative and others about whether anyone on site actually understood German. To this, she always replied that the project leader had asked her to make these translations. However, it was also evident that she enjoyed the task. Languages and translations were her specialties in the management team, where she was a newcomer with no knowledge about construction work. When I asked the project leader why he wanted German translations, he laughingly replied that that had been a joke. While it was indeed unlikely that there was a need for German translations in the workplace, I was still surprised that the status of Pia's interpretation work was so ambiguous. Sometimes it was presented as very important – and it was something she clearly took professional pride in – while at other times it was presented as irrelevant or even 'a joke'. Regardless, the workplace and other team members could put Pia's translations to good use. For example, the foreman who had instructed her to make only Norwegian versions had a meeting with some external partners one day. They enquired about whether written information was available in more languages and, suddenly, the foreman seemed happy to show them Pia's English version of a site map. I observed this moment, but I don't know if anyone ever told Pia that it was a good thing she had decided to defy the foreman's instructions.

Six months into the project, the contractor got a new daily leader who decided to restructure the company's business model. This entailed the axing of all temporary staff. As the secretary – a role that is relegated to temporary workers due to its low status and lack of recognition – Pia was fired.

Quintus

by Rachel Mairs

About 1800 years ago, somewhere in the neighbourhood of present-day Boldog, Slovakia, a man named Quintus Atilius Primus died and was commemorated by his family in a short Latin inscription. His tombstone was then reused in the mediaeval Church of the Assumption, where it remained hidden under a layer of plaster until uncovered during renovations in the 1970s. The preservation of Atilius's tombstone at Boldog is important because it makes him one of the very few interpreters from the Roman Empire whom we know by name, and about whose life and career we are able to say much at all.

> Q(uintus) Atilius sp(urius) f(ilius) Vot(uria) Primus inter<p>rex leg(ionis) XV idem (centurio) negotiator an(norum) LXXX h(ic) s(itus) e(st) Q(uintus) Atilius Cog(i)tatus Atilia Q(uinti) l(iberta) Fausta Privatus et Martialis hered(es) l(iberti?) p(osuerunt)

> Quintus Atilius Primus, illegitimate, of the tribe Voturia, interpreter of the Fifteenth Legion, centurion of the same, trader, aged 80, lies here. Quintus Atilius Cogitatus and Atilia Fausta, freedwoman of Quintus, Privatus and Martialis, his heirs, freedmen, placed (this monument).

About 50 kilometres from Boldog was the Roman fort of Carnuntum, on the Danube in present-day Austria, where the Fifteenth Legion was stationed for most of the first and early second centuries. Like all Roman legions, however, it could be moved to trouble spots around the empire. From 63 to 71, it was stationed in Syria. The legions also recruited from across the empire, so the fort at Carnuntum was home to people from across Europe, North Africa and the Middle East, who brought with them their languages and religions. Despite this diversity, the only official language of the army was Latin: it was used in all official documents and inscriptions. As well as widespread multilingualism, interpreters would have been essential for the army camp and its town to function. The elite Roman authors who composed most of the literary and historical works which survive to the present day were, on the whole, uninterested in everyday linguistic mediation of this sort. Upper-class Romans were educated in Greek as well as Latin, and took a certain interest in written translation, but the mechanisms – and the very necessity – of mediating between spoken, low-status languages were neglected.

Our interpreter's name, Atilius, indicates that he came from the Atilia family, who were originally from Aquileia, but by this period, because of their business interests in the amber trade between the Baltic and the Adriatic, had spread out across this route. There are inscriptions for other members of the clan, probably only very distant relations of our Atilius, from Carnuntum at the same period. Given his family origins, Atilius was most likely a native speaker of Latin and, if he had had any formal education, may also have known some Greek. In his life in the Danube region and career in the army, however, he would have come into everyday contact with speakers of a vast range of languages: belonging to the Germanic, Celtic, Iranian and probably Baltic and Slavic families in the locality, and also to Afro-Asiatic among the soldiers.

Atilius's inscription does not tell us exactly which languages he used or how he acquired them. The fact that he is illegitimate is significant. Roman soldiers were forbidden from marrying during their active service, but this did not, of course, mean that they were celibate. Some soldiers, in fact, formed stable family units and had children with women whom they may not have been able to legally marry, but whom they and their comrades recognised as their 'wives'. After they left the army – if they survived that long – soldiers were free to marry their partners and legitimate their children. The fact that Atilius had a full Roman name and tribal membership suggests that he was recognised by his father, even though he was not legitimate (because his father, as a soldier, could not marry). Of his mother, we know nothing. She could have been a local girl from Carnuntum, or anywhere in the empire, and have raised her son speaking her own language in the home, as well as his father's Latin.

Atilius's family background, although tersely related, tells us a lot about how he came to be a member of a multiethnic, multilingual milieu, where interpreting was important, and where he might have acquired the languages necessary in his familial and professional life. Soldiers sometimes had relationships with women who were their slaves. Reading between the lines of Atilius's epitaph, this appears to have been the case for him. Atilia Fausta was his 'freedwoman', his ex-slave. Freed slaves typically took part of their former master's name as their own, which is why she is 'Atilia'. We do not know her birth name or ethnic origin but, like Atilius's mother, she could have been from anywhere in the Roman Empire or its neighbouring territories. Atilia's position in the inscription suggests very strongly that she was also his wife. She may have been in a relationship with him for a long time, even during his army days. Quintus Atilius Cogitatus, named first in the inscription, is their son. (We cannot say anything much about his other heirs, Privatus and Martialis, who do not bear his name.) The women in Atilius's life – his wife and mother – are therefore likely to have been native speakers of languages other than Latin, explaining how he acquired and maintained his multilingualism. We do not know what language(s) he and Atilia Fausta spoke to their son, but it seems probable that their home was a multilingual one.

Eighty is an unusually ripe age for someone to live to at this period, especially a man running all the risks that came with a military career. Roman soldiers served for 25 years, although centurions like Atilius sometimes chose to serve longer. He therefore lived for some decades after his retirement from active service. Retired soldiers received a payment upon discharge, which could be used for investment in a business or property. This start-up capital may have been what allowed Atilius to set himself up as a trader. There would certainly have been plenty of opportunities for this in and around Carnuntum. As well as routes supplying the fort and its town, there was the north–south 'Amber Route' running through the region, which Atilius's own family at Aquileia were involved in. The linguistic dimension is also important. Atilius's training as an interpreter would have given him experience mediating transactions and relationships, even during his time in the army. As well as using other languages in his career, he was exposed to them in his personal life, from his mother and his wife. He was therefore in an ideal position to prosper as a trader: multilingual, with army and local connections.

When Atilius died, his family did for him what countless other military families did for their loved ones: they set up a Latin inscription, with concise details of his career and personal ties. These inscriptions are formulaic. They are almost always in Latin, no matter what the ethnic origin of the deceased, and they always give the same kind of information: name, paternity, tribe, military rank, legion, age, names of heirs. Very often, these inscriptions lack a personal touch. They also tend to omit the diverse ethno-linguistic backgrounds of the people commemorating and commemorated. Ex-slaves, like Atilia Fausta, are given the Roman names of their former masters. The mothers of the illegitimate children of Roman soldiers, like Atilius himself, are erased.

Very rarely, we get a glimpse of something more. A tombstone from near Hadrian's Wall, from a little later than Atilius's on the Danube, is in both Latin and Palmyrene. It commemorates a woman with the Roman name Regina, but who comes from a native British tribe. She was the wife and ex-slave of a man called Barates, from Palmyra in Syria. Like Atilius, the case of Barates and Regina shows us that the Roman army was a place of intense ethno-linguistic interaction. Although Atilius is extremely rare in being described as an interpreter on his tombstone, the role would have been performed – perhaps unrecognised and unvalued – by thousands of others in the Roman Empire.

Roland

by Ebenezer Tedjouong

When I met him some 10 years ago, he had just retired from the UN, where he had served as English reviser (a senior translator who reviews other translators' work) and team leader (in interpretation) at the International Criminal Tribunal for Rwanda in Arusha, Tanzania. We worked on the same jury during the entrance, end-of-semester and final exams at the Advanced School of Translators and Interpreters (ASTI) at the University of Buea, Cameroon. Every colleague, Cameroonian and non-Cameroonian alike, from East, Central or Southern Africa, fondly called him Mzee, which is the Swahili title for dignitaries, earned by position, character or achievement. Given my inquisitive nature, I never stopped gathering facts, which led me to the conclusion that Roland Ngong is a Mzee of conference interpretation in Africa, and the world at large.

In his early days at the University of Yaoundé (then known as the Federal University of Cameroon), Mzee got excited about being fluent in French and chose bilingual letters (English and French) as his field of study, thus abandoning law, which would otherwise have been his first choice. Being one of the best students in the translation course, he was selected by Mbassi Manga, a renowned lecturer, to feature among the privileged few who did the combined honours in English and French. Then followed studies at Georgetown University in Washington, DC, where he graduated as conference interpreter with the late King Ondoua (a Cameroonian professional conference interpreter of the first generation who died in his booth in the 1990s).

Roland Ngong started working as an in-house interpreter at the Office of the President of the Republic of Cameroon in 1974. He was bent on excelling professionally, on being a good interpreter or translator or reviser. In those early days, he shared an office with Tening Mongwa, then personal interpreter of President Amadou Ahidjo, who was a source of comfort and motivation for him in his quest for excellence. Marvelled by the prestige and performance of a senior figure who often travelled with the President of the Republic, Roland nursed the ambition of emulating Mongwa's example. A few years later, Roland's remarkable performance had earned President Ahidjo's trust, so much so that he often insisted on working specifically with him. He then fully replaced Mongwa when he was appointed attaché to the President. At this point, however, seeing Mongwa's career path – from being an interpreter to being granted an administrative position – had a 'cold shower effect' on Roland, as the French would put it. Mzee was torn between continuing to work at the President's Office, where the likely outcome would be leaving the profession and embarking on an administrative career, or sticking to his initial commitment to the profession by becoming a freelance interpreter.

Turning his back on a path that would lead to becoming an *attaché de cabinet, chargé de mission* or *conseiller technique*, Roland dared, when it was not conventional practice, to resign from his position as English reviser and head of the English translation service, as well as chief interpreter at the Presidency of the Republic, to become a freelance translator and interpreter. After three letters of resignation and having to refund expenses incurred by the government for his internship at the Commission of European Communities in Luxembourg, he was finally allowed to leave. After one of the audiences, President Ahidjo asked him, 'Donc vous voulez nous quitter maintenant?' ('So you want to leave us now?'). Roland said, 'Quitter comment, Excellence?' ('What do you mean by "leaving", Excellence?'] and the President replied, 'Oui j'ai vu votre lettre de démission ... j'ai donné mon accord' ('Yes I saw your resignation letter ... I approved it'). Roland literally skipped out of the President's Office, extremely happy. In those days, it took a decision by the President of the Republic for any high-ranking civil servant to resign from their position. Any person resigning faced the risk of being perceived as a traitor, especially when this person had knowledge of confidential files, as any interpreter normally would.

Before leaving the Presidency, Roland Ngong had begun advertising his services. He joined King Ondoua, who had himself just resigned from the Cameroonian parliament, known as the National Assembly. They created a consultancy named Conference Services Limited. Business boomed as the number of meetings they assisted with on the continent kept increasing. Roland, now a father of three, started noticing that his travels did not leave him enough time to take care of his family. It was now time to search for a permanent job to help him develop a work–life balance, a job that would enable him bring up his children morally, as any father would want.

After some months of job hunting, Roland landed in Addis Ababa, where he had been recruited by the Organisation of African Unity (OAU). He spent 12–13 years with the OAU, interpreting all over the continent, including in high-level meetings with presidents such as the Togolese Gnassingbé Eyadéma and Ivorian Félix Houphouët-Boigny. Roland appears to have been one of the closest and most stable conference interpreters under Salim Ahmed Salim, then Secretary-General of the OAU. Once again, however, business did not allow Mzee to have enough time for his family. He therefore meditated on seeking a new job as in-house interpreter with an international organisation, which could grant him stability and a clear career path in interpreting.

Known for his self-confidence and discipline in meeting preparation, as well as versatility of mind, Roland Ngong never lacked grease in his elbows, and was soon to fly to greater heights. In 1997, he left the OAU for the UN in Arusha, where he remained until his retirement in 2009.

While at the International Tribunal in Arusha, Mzee started studying law, his original passion, at the University of South Africa. But when he was made leader of the interpretation team, it entailed so much work that he had little or no time to pursue his studies. He was forced to drop them after two and a half years. Nevertheless, the insight that he developed gave him an edge over his colleagues, who sometimes struggled with the complexities of legal concepts and jargon.

Though Roland retired from the UN in 2009, he never fully retired from the profession. He is and remains an interpreter – a freelance interpreter. In this capacity, he serves meetings for the African Union, the World Health Organization, the African Union Advisory Board on Corruption in Arusha, the International Monetary Fund, the World Bank and the Pan African Parliament, to name just a few. Between meetings, Roland used to live in Kumbo, some 80 kilometres from Bamenda in northwest Cameroon, where he enjoyed trekking in the mountains of his hilly homeland. Sadly, in 2016, a sociopolitical crisis forced Roland out of Kumbo. Separatists have been claiming the independence of English-speaking Cameroon, leading the country into a civil-war-like situation. Since then, Mzee has become an internally displaced person and lives in a town where trekking is no longer convenient.

Roland started interpreting 45 years ago, and his life is full of stories and anecdotes. No surprise that, whenever people gather around him for 5 to 10 minutes, he tells a lot of jokes and all sorts of anecdotes from his rich experience which render everyone spellbound. Any encounter with Mzee is a party. As I was interviewing him somewhere in the seaside town of Limbe, I enjoyed his ability to paint the past and inspire hope in the younger generation as much as the fresh sea breeze. An easy-going, trustworthy and reliable fellow, Mzee incarnates the personality of the perfect interpreter. He has thus worked with clients at both the grassroots and the summit level. He is no stranger to prominent African political leaders, including, besides those already mentioned, Ghana's Jerry Rawlings, even Nelson Mandela.

Full of humility and very objective in his appraisal, Mzee knows that his peers respect him for his performance. Those who are younger, including the students whom he has had the opportunity to work with, make him slightly uncomfortable. Why? Because sometimes, in the booth, a former student might turn to him and ask, 'Excuse me sir, was that okay?' and 'What do you think?', whereas Mzee prefers to consider his former students simply as colleagues. I was not so lucky to be his student, but our collaboration in teaching at the Advanced School of Translators and Interpreters has let me discover a man of great dignity.

To those whose desire is to succeed in conference interpreting, Mzee repeats over and over:

You have to have self-confidence. That's number one. Number two: you have to prepare your work. That is, before you go for a meeting, you try as much as you can to have as much information on the purpose of the meeting, what will be discussed. You can even Google things about the meeting. You prepare yourself; you prepare your terminology notes so that you are fully conversant in what you are going to be talking about; that is preparation for the meeting. Number three: you must be cooperative in the booth. You have to cooperate with your colleague. Help your colleague in case of difficulty and don't give the impression that you are undermining them. Because I have noticed something: when you work well with a colleague, usually they are impressed. Particularly if you are performing well, they are impressed. So, they are the people who will tell another organisation, 'Oh you know, I worked with this man and he is very very good'. You'll be surprised what kind of organisations will get in touch with you.... Then, don't show off: 'I am the best, I am the this, I am the that'. There is no need for that. Just be a nice man, be a decent person, do your work properly, prepare yourself for the work, don't make people hate you for no reason. That's about it. Yeah ... that's about it, you know? But before you go into the market, particularly to this freelancing, you have to advertise yourself, you have to publicise yourself and your skills. You have to, to the extent possible, circulate your CV, and usually, when you are writing to an organisation, you tailor your CV to suit the cause of the organisation.... Next week I'm being interviewed by TV5 on promoting interpretation, publicising interpretation, 'comme une profession inconnue, même dans les pays développés' ['as if it was an unknown profession, even in developed countries'].

Thank you, Mzee!

Saeed

by Beatriz Lorente

I heard about Saeed before I met him. There's a student, the teachers told me, who is difficult and *mayabang*. He thinks highly of himself and does not want to accept feedback. He can't wait to go to the next chapter of his textbook even if we insist that he should review. The teachers had nicknamed him Mr Bascomb, a main character in Exploring English, a series of English-language textbooks widely used in the English school in Baguio, the Philippines, where I am doing fieldwork. I am told that when I meet Saeed, I will understand why they've given him this nickname.

I finally meet Saeed on the third day of my fieldwork. I first see him at the main office. Dressed in dark-blue jeans and a collared shirt, he looks serious as he talks to Ma'am Joy, the school's academic head, and Teacher Paul, one of the head teachers, about changing the textbooks they have assigned to him. Like the Mr Bascomb in the textbook series, he is rotund and he has a black mustache and round eyeglasses. After I introduce myself, I ask him why he doesn't like his textbooks. All of his textbooks are photocopies, he says, and these are probably illegal. He picks up one, shows me the page with the publication information and says that the textbook is quite old. It is not published by Oxford or Cambridge, and he thinks that its structure, with the chapters revolving around recurring characters and stories, is for young learners and not university students like him.

Mr Bascomb is a rich banker. Saeed is not a banker but the Filipino teachers think he is rich. He rents his own apartment, instead of sharing one with other students. He paid up front for his three months of English classes, in full. He does not like to eat at the makeshift *turo-turo* at the back of the building where the school is located. Instead, he buys food from the nearest convenience store, a 7–11, or he gets it delivered from McDonald's or KFC (he was sure they were halal, he told me). Saeed is also one of a handful of Saudi students at the school and this differentiates him from the other 'Arabic students' who also live in Saudi Arabia and speak Arabic but who have Yemeni, Libyan, Syrian, Egyptian, Sudanese and other nationalities. I soon learn just how much Saeed's nationality makes him different from the other 'Arabic students'. Saeed is a fourth-year pharmacy student at one of the prestigious universities in Saudi Arabia and he says he needs general English because private companies look for people who can speak English. The non-Saudi 'Arabic students' are learning English because the new Saudization policy is making it increasingly untenable for them and their families to live in Saudi Arabia. Universities in Saudi Arabia are too difficult to get into and too expensive, so they hope that learning English will allow them to study in an English-speaking country, perhaps the Philippines. Saeed had filled his day with English classes, from 8am to 5pm, five days a week, with a break for lunch and another break in the early afternoon. He was considered a 'serious student', like the South Korean students who also filled their days with English classes and unlike some Saudis who took just enough classes to qualify for the Special Study Permit and were mainly in the Philippines for a 'good time'. But Saeed could also afford to take so many English classes. The other 'Arabic students', especially those with Yemeni passports, tended to enroll for just two or three, or sometimes even only one class per day, because that was what they could afford. Before coming to Baguio, Saeed had gone to the UK and then to Malaysia for short English courses. Those countries were more advanced than the Philippines, he said, but no other place beat the value for money he was currently getting. In the UK and Malaysia, all of his English lessons were group classes. In Baguio, all of his classes were one-on-one (the prevailing teaching format of English-language schools in Baguio) or 'person-to-person'. Besides, he liked how people in Baguio understood his English. Even the itinerant vendor who hawked brooms in his neighborhood spoke to him in English. The brooms were dirt cheap, he said. The vendor walked around trying to sell his wares the whole day and he probably earned very little. Come to think of it, his teachers were probably not earning a lot and one of them was even supporting her daughter on her own. How, he asked me, could people live on so little?

There were some teachers who thought differently about Saeed. Teacher Joyce did not teach Saeed; she thought he was annoying but they constantly joked with each other. Other teachers thought that his frequent interjections of 'Piece of cake!' was his way of making himself appear more confident than he actually was. One of these teachers held their one-on-one classes in the faculty room because her room, like the rooms of most of the teachers in the school, was too small for Saeed's big frame. The first and only time they had class there, she had to keep the door open so Saeed could stretch his legs. Saeed liked hanging out in the faculty room. He did his homework, surfed the internet and chatted with the teachers who also hung out there. The teachers did not really like Saeed hanging out in their faculty room but they tolerated it. There was nowhere else where Mr Bascomb would fit.

Saeed was an earnest participant in my fieldwork. He volunteered to be observed while he was in class. He offered suggestions as to whom I should interview, laughingly differentiating between students with 'normal English' and 'abnormal English' (where he included himself). One afternoon, when I asked Fahad, another Saudi student, whether we could chat about his experiences learning English in Baguio, Saeed happened to pass by in the school corridor. He stopped, listened to our conversation, heard Fahad ask me what I meant by 'research', and jumped in, in Arabic. The only words I could understand from their conversation were 'research' and 'Swissa'. When Fahad agreed (in English) to meet me the next day, Saeed turned to him and said something in Arabic that made Fahad bring out his mobile phone and enter the date and time of our meeting. Later, when I asked Saeed what he had said to Fahad, his response to me was a gruff 'I make sure he comes to the interview'.

In my third week of fieldwork, I asked Saeed if we could go over the Overseas Workers Welfare Administration (OWWA) manual I had that was entitled *Arabic Language and Culture Familiarization*. The manual was used in a language training program the OWWA had designed for Filipino domestic workers bound for Arabic-speaking countries. For an earlier research project, I had sat down with other fluent Arabic-speakers in order to interpret the manual but I had never asked an Arabic-speaker from Saudi Arabia, the number-one destination of transnational Filipino domestic workers, to interpret it. The manual had four columns: a transliteration of the Arabic word, Filipino, English, Arabic (written in Arabic). I asked Saeed whether the English translations of the Arabic expressions were accurate. We spent a lot of time in the section 'Household Chores'. The English translations of these Arabic expressions had always sounded like commands to me. The first and third columns of the section looked like this:

Qatti'iyl basal	Cut the onions
Qatti'iyl attamaatim	Cut the tomatoes
Qatti'iy addajaaj	Cut the chicken

Yes, Saeed said, the written Arabic was accurate and the transliteration was okay. Yes, Arabic marks for gender. See, the 'iy' sound means that the one being addressed is a woman. These expressions are normal, he told me. They are not rude or impolite. If his mother were to tell him to cut onions, she would use these words. She would not say: 'Please cut the onions'. What if his mother asked his father to cut onions, would she use the same words? 'Ha!', he laughed, 'my father does not cook! I cook. A little. Piece of cake!' When I asked him whether his family employed domestic workers from the Philippines, he said that their maids used to be from Indonesia and that now they're from Africa. 'The Filipino maids in Saudi', he whispered to me, 'they earn more than the teachers here'.

Towards the end of my month of fieldwork at the school, I ask Ma'am Joy what happens to Mr Bascomb. She told me that in the fifth and last book of the series, Mr Bascomb runs for mayor on a platform of improving the economy of the city. He wants to bring in more business and more jobs. He plans to build a toy factory in one of the parks. He spends a lot on his campaign. He runs against Otis Jackson, an artist who wants to protect the environment and save the park. Otis Jackson has little money but his campaign has a lot of volunteers. The book ends with the town's citizens voting but it does not include the election results so no one knows whether Mr Bascomb won or lost.

At the school's main office, almost a month after I first meet Saeed, I overhear him telling a teacher, 'I wait for you, Teacher Joyce'. Teacher Joyce stayed on in the school after everyone else had gone home so she could teach a few Korean students online in the evening. Usually, Teacher Paul stayed behind to keep her company. Saeed had also started to stay behind. He did not like being alone in his apartment. He liked finishing his homework in the faculty room and he enjoyed joking around with Teacher Joyce. That day, Teacher Paul had to go home early and so Teacher Joyce was in the office, asking if anyone else was going home as late as she was. No one else was, except Saeed: 'I wait for you, Teacher Joyce. I do my homework.'

'Bespreeeeeeeeeeen', I heard Teacher Joyce say in an exasperated but affectionate tone. 'Bigla akong nagka-bespren ng Arabo' ('I suddenly have a best friend who is an Arab').

Sandra

by Verena Krausneker and Sandra Schügerl

This text is based on a conversation between the authors in Austrian Sign Language. Verena Krausneker turned it into a German text and the two authors translated the chapter into English.

When Sandra was a teenager, still in gymnasium, she already translated letters for her deaf mother from German into Austrian Sign Language (Österreichische Gebärdensprache, ÖGS). For deaf people, the written language of the country they live in is a second language, and many do not fully master it. So, written texts are visually accessible, but in many cases are not fully understood. Sandra, being a high school student, had achieved greater mastery of German than her mum, and thus she provided translations. "Translating," Sandra says, now in her thirties, "is therefore an ongoing process and part of my everyday life."

In Austria, there are about two handfuls of teachers who are sign language users and deaf. Even in specialized schools where pupils with hearing impairments study, there are scarcely any linguistic and social role models, because most teachers are hearing. Most learned ÖGS very late in life, as a foreign language, if at all. Sandra is one of the very few deaf teachers in Austria, and she has an immensely important role, both for the children and teenagers she teaches, and for her colleagues. But Sandra is also a sign of progress for the entire system of deaf education and a key player, because the system has for decades actively excluded people like her (through audistic admission criteria for teacher training, demanding for instance that all applicants be able to sing and play an instrument). Nevertheless,

Sandra the deaf teacher has recently decided to become a self-employed interpreter.

Sandra was born into a deaf family, surrounded by visually oriented people using a visual language, ÖGS, in their daily life. This was the first language Sandra acquired. German was the second, and also the language of her schooling. In her youth, she was fascinated by interpreters and watched their simultaneous interpreting in awe. After successfully passing matriculation, she enquired if she, a deaf person, could train in the field of interpreting. She thought she could cooperate with hearing interpreters, but the answer was a very clear "No."

Therefore, she started to train as a teacher, but very soon learned that, at University of Hamburg, deaf people could train as interpreters, and immediately applied there too. For two years, she simultaneously studied in Vienna to be a teacher and in Hamburg to be an interpreter and translator. The seminars at the University of Hamburg were conducted on a part-time basis, and Sandra received financial support from the Austrian Federal Ministry of Social Affairs to cover tuition. She used her private funds to pay for transport and accommodation. Monday to Friday, Sandra studied in Vienna to become a teacher, and on weekends in Hamburg to become an interpreter. This double load may not sound easy, but she was young, ambitious and hungry for knowledge, and now says that "studying in Hamburg was actually refreshing."

When, in 2014, she successfully graduated in Hamburg, there was – just like today – a severe shortage of sign language interpreters. (As of 2019, there were a total of 8.7 million people in Austria, 8000 of them deaf sign language users, and about 130 active professional sign language interpreters.) But again, Sandra was told: "No demand [for you]." Back then, no one could imagine where and how to put a deaf interpreter to use. So Sandra started working as a teacher and made it her business to actively raise awareness of the need and benefits of deaf interpreters. She knew that deaf interpreters were successfully working in many countries, and she spread this message, both among the deaf community and among interpreters.

There are many situations where a deaf person is quicker to understand what a client is signing, for example if the client has a sign language other than ÖGS as their first language. Hearing interpreters have usually studied ÖGS as a foreign language and rarely know any other sign languages. A deaf interpreter can much more readily understand a signer with a strong accent from another sign language, or with minimal competence in ÖGS.

Or if the client is a deaf person with learning disabilities and uses a very simplified form of ÖGS, a deaf interpreter can adapt to this register much more easily.

Or when clients are under exceptional psychological stress and utter parts of sentences in a manner which may be difficult to understand for hearing signers, with slurs and breaks and unfinished sentences....

A deaf interpreter will also be an asset when dealing with clients who have very little formal education or only very basic German competence, as well as clients who are very old or who live isolated in rural areas. As native signers, they usually understand more variants and dialects, or registers of their sign language. Apart from this, deaf interpreters can translate written texts into marvelously clear signed texts.

Still, Sandra encountered pushback: "There were a lot of discussions," she recalls. Hearing sign language interpreters were opposed because they were not familiar with the idea of working with deaf interpreters and did not see the need for it. Sandra had the impression that they feared their work would be under scrutiny, something that very rarely happens to sign language interpreters, because there is usually no one present who can understand both languages and pass judgment on their work. Usually, one side cannot understand the signed output and the other side cannot hear the spoken output.

But then, her first assignment came along, thanks to a few interpreters who were more open and willing to include her in jobs where it was clear from the start that the deaf client would be hard to understand, "and I slowly found my role," she explains.

In 2015, with the Eurovision Song Contest being held in Vienna, there was a breakthrough in awareness of what deaf interpreters are able to do when Austrian public television (ORF) decided make the entire show fully accessible; not only would the presenters be interpreted, but the songs would be translated as well. Sandra worked on the show as part of a team of three hearing and deaf translators, plus five deaf performers. The team worked on over 40 songs with a focus on storytelling, spending an average of three hours on each song to deliver a translation of content and purpose. The translators then handed the signed texts over to the deaf performers so they could practice. The entire three-day event was designed to be barrier-free for the deaf. Much acknowledged in the sign language community, the event finally made publicly visible that outstanding interpreter quality is possible only when done by deaf–hearing teams.

Sandra carried on teaching, was active as a lecturer in teacher training and interpreted from time to time. But she was constantly questioning whether she was doing the right thing as an interpreter. She discussed and reflected upon it and she finally decided to apply for the European Master in Sign Language Interpreting (EUMASLI), a degree that was not available to deaf people at a German-speaking university. English competence was one of the admission criteria for this training program, because courses are taught in English. For Sandra, this meant mastering a third language which she could not hear, but only read and write.

In 2017, Sandra was accepted to the Master program, began to study and attended the EUMASLI lectures, which took place alternatingly at the three cooperating universities in three different countries. EUMASLI students are mainly hearing, and lectures are mostly delivered in spoken English, so Sandra always had to bring along her team of Austrian hearing interpreters to sign the spoken lectures in ÖGS. The logistical, financial and organizational complexity was considerable, but she successfully graduated in 2019.

Apart from improving her working language English, she says, the biggest effect of EUMASLI was the realization that "I was doing everything right as an interpreter." The decisions she takes in simultaneous interpretation, her reflections on her role in many complex situations … she is more certain today that she is on the right path.

Sandra thinks and dreams in Austrian Sign Language. Her everyday life is characterized by four languages: ÖGS, written German, written English and International Sign. Sandra is now ready for conference interpreting in international settings; she can read the English papers to prepare and she can interpret into International Sign. But in the course of the last two years, she has noticed that translating interests her more. When she translates written into signed texts, "I can give everything I've got. I can really work on it and produce a super-clean, elegant text."

In Austria, most sign language interpreting is financed by the Ministry of Social Affairs. For deaf interpreters, working in a team with a hearing colleague is essential, so the Ministry covers the cost of the hearing interpreter, as a kind of professional expense. It is a rather odd construction, but after everything that Sandra Schügerl has achieved in shifting people's opinions, she does not mind that her colleagues are paid to "assist" her, and not as professional interpreters in a team of equals. On the contrary, she has recently decided to quit her jobs in teaching and teacher training in order to fully immerse herself in the life of a self-employed deaf interpreter.

Online resources

European Master in Sign Language Interpreting: https://www.eumasli.eu.
Eurovision Song Contest medley of sign language interpreters: https://www.youtube.com/watch?v=jVLbupPINUE.
Eurovision Song Contest short with Sandra: https://www.facebook.com/evamaria.hinterwirth/videos/962036723840629.
University of Hamburg Deaf Sign Language Interpreters master's course: https://www.zfw.uni-hamburg.de/weiterbildung/sprache-kunst-kultur/taube-gebaerdensprachdolmetscher.html.

Tulay

by Tulay Caglitutuncigil

It was around 8pm. I had just arrived home from a conference. I had been working all day in the booth and I was tired,
thinking only about a nice dinner, wine and my sofa. This is
normally how you feel at the end of a week-long conference if
you are working as an interpreter. When it is over, you feel a
deep relief. You also feel exhausted. I sometimes envy the interpreters living in Brussels, commuting to a European institution
every day. I wonder if they go to work by bike. Maybe they live
so close to work that they just walk? In any case it is not like
living in Istanbul, that's for sure. In Istanbul, there are nearly
20 million people living in the same city, and if you live on the
Asian side, you need to cross the Bosporus to go to work, as
most of the conferences are organised on the European side.
(This might sound crazy, but in Istanbul in general, people live
in Asia and commute to Europe for work.) While I was lost in
these thoughts, I received a call from an interpreting agency.
There was a last-minute government mission and the delegation
needed a Spanish-English-Turkish-speaking interpreter to go to
Africa the next day. As I was asking about the details (How many
days? What time is the flight tomorrow? Where will we stay?), I
was coping with my inner voice (Do I need a vaccine? Maybe I
should leave the keys with my neighbour so they can feed my
cat? What should I wear? What about the dinner party that I
am supposed to attend tomorrow?). Being an interpreter means
that you must always be available, and you need to adapt your
life accordingly. Your plans with family and friends are always
subject to last-minute change, and you always need to have your
hand luggage prepared. This is how I have been living for more
than 10 years. But I was not worried about the flight or the trip

itself; I was worried about the delegation and I had very good reason to be worried. Interpreting for the government in Turkey is like walking through a minefield. You need to be available all the time and forget about proper working hours. You might be working until 1am due to last-minute changes in the schedule, and you might have a couple hours of sleep and take off at 5am for another country. It is all about flexibility and patience, a lot of patience. And it is all about being invisible, especially if you are a woman interpreter.

The next day, I woke up early to fly to Ankara, because the delegation was flying on a government airplane from the capital. They picked me at the airport and took me to the meeting point. They guided me to the main office, where I met the secretary of the delegation. His first question was whether I had something more appropriate to wear. I wondered what 'more appropriate' meant. I was wearing a black dress coming down below my knees, thick black socks, black shoes and a formal jacket. And he was asking me if had a suit with me, preferably a black one. I am sure that he was very disappointed when I said no, but there was nothing to do. His Majesty preferred working with men, he explained, and when he worked with women he preferred to see them in a black suit. Honestly, I was not surprised to hear that. In recent years, almost all government delegations had preferred to work with male interpreters during their trips. This increasing 'androcentrism', or in other words disappearance of women interpreters on government trips, was an increasing problem for women like myself, as we were losing the market because of a gender-based segregation. Most of the time, officials preferred working with men even if they lacked interpreting skills, just because they did not want to see women in the delegation.

There I was, sitting on a sofa, trying to hide my legs and trying to find the best place to rest my hands and arms. I wanted to look calm and confident, when I was annoyed and nervous inside. It was 1pm, and they told me that our flight was at 10pm; they just wanted to be sure that I was not late by ordering me to the office nine hours before the take-off. Perfect! After nine long hours, they finally told me we were heading to the airport. Nobody wanted to give me any information about the visit. There were many people rushing around, holding papers, accreditations, but they were reluctant to provide me with any information. Finally, on the plane, I got a copy of the agenda (which would change a hundred times, of course). I took a deep breath and started reading the documents to have a better insight into this official trip. I hoped that everything would be easy and smooth, but I was wrong. We were 13 people travelling on a plane designed for six passengers for seven hours, without taking any proper rest because there was no space, not even to stretch our legs. Only the 'VIPs' were able to sleep, while the rest tried to find a small space to rest their heads for a while. Not surprisingly, I was the only woman in the group, apart from a woman agent (it is obligatory to have a woman police officer in each delegation). When we arrived at our destination, it was around 2am, and it was 4 by the time I was in the hotel bed. We were supposed to go to an official ceremony at 8am, which meant that I woke up at 6.30 because there were one-on-one meetings before the ceremony. By noon, I could hardly stand on my feet. I was tired and restless, trying to keep calm and not to lose my temper, but it was very hard. There were rumours that our bosses were planning to stay for two more nights; I had other assignments that week and had to fly back. There were no direct flights between this African country and Turkey, and I was obliged to fly back on the government plane. I was annoyed by the way that they treated me, and tired of standing for hours and hours because they made me stand at the door even though they did not need translation. They did not even bother to ask me if I had had breakfast or lunch. Everything about this trip was so wrong that finally I started asking myself existential questions, such as what I was doing with my life or if this profession was ruining it. I kept asking myself these questions even after flying back to Turkey the following day. Nevertheless, I would forget about this experience in few days, after working with a company who showed me respect and gratitude for the job that I did for them. In fact, I must say that I mostly work with a lot of nice, understanding and respectful clients. Most of them understand the difficulty of our job and they do their best to provide us with the physical and social conditions that we need in order to offer an excellent service. Respectful and healthy communication makes everything smooth and easy, and we, as interpreters, know this better than anyone else.

In this short contribution, I have tried to explain the experience of a woman interpreter working for the Turkish government. I wanted to underline that interpreting requires dealing with power asymmetries, and even if we are supposed to be invisible, an interpreter is not exempt from racial, social, economic and gender identity. Nevertheless, not everything is black. I have been working as a conference interpreter since 2005, and in spite of its challenges, I love my job. I enjoy learning something new every day, having freedom, meeting new people, travelling around the world and, most of all, I enjoy working as a bridge between cultures and languages. Interpreting is a highly intellectual exercise that requires skills beyond fluency in two or more languages. It requires stress management, problem-solving skills and knowledge of science, arts, politics, law, medicine, nature and many other fields. A good interpreter has a curious brain and loves research, reading and learning. I am passionate about this intellectual feature of my job and I know that I am a good professional. And I also know that sometimes, the simple fact that you exist, you breathe, that you do an excellent job is the best way to stand up for your rights. Everything is subject to change and we live in a dynamic world; governments will change, politics may vary, but we will keep building bridges between countries, cultures and people. This is the essence of our job, which is one of the oldest professions in the world. Therefore, I keep working as an enthusiastic and hardworking professional who will always stand up for her rights, even when it means defending her right to wear a dress and red lipstick.

Yang

by Biao Xiang

'Work is a medium', said Yang Fuyou, or Ramadan, as he is known to his Arabic-speaking clients from the Middle East and North Africa, in his usual soft but firm tone. Slim, fair-skinned, and slightly crook-backed, Yang is shy in public but becomes talkative and even mischievous in private. 'In the Arabic world, there is a saying: "Keep one eye on the sacred text, keep the other eye on society [secular world]". The present life is a training ground for the next. We sow seeds in this life for our afterlife', Yang explains. Work is important because 'work is full of challenges. The more difficulties we go through, the more faithful we become'. Work is thus a medium between the secular and the religious, between wealth and meaning, and between the self and Allah.

Yang's work is literally a medium. He is an Arabic–Chinese translator and a buying agent who sources goods from China for his foreign clients. to be sold in other parts of the Global South. There were about 4000 translators in Guangzhou, a metropolis in south China, close to Hong Kong, at any time between 2010 and 2016 (the number dropped afterwards due to a decline in trade). Most of them were men, aged between 25 and 40, and had migrated from north-west China, which is the heartland of the Muslim population (the Hui). They started coming to Guangzhou in the early 1990s, when sizeable numbers of Arabic-speaking traders travelled to south China to purchase low-price everyday consumer goods, ranging from toys to furniture. Completely new in China, the traders promised high pay to whoever could help with languages.

An interpreter's job, Yang insisted, is much more than finding equivalence across languages. The real challenge lies in, as Yang put it, 'understanding Chinese in Chinese, then explaining Arabic in Arabic':

> The [foreign] clients have many questions [when bargaining with the supplier]. Sometimes it takes one hour just to cut down the price by one RMB [US$0.15]. It is not easy to understand what the Chinese suppliers mean when they say that they can't reduce the price, or they say that the product must be modified if the clients want it to be delivered earlier. Are they bluffing, or are they telling the truth? How much truth is in the truth? We have to explain to our clients till they nod and seal the deal.

Translation is also an act of diplomacy. In low-end trade, where every party is price-sensitive and the process can be unpredictable, both the suppliers and the purchasers can easily become agitated. Translation should be selective and constructive. 'Don't translate the useless comments. Try to stop them from making these comments if you see one is coming.'

Yang had become increasingly interested in existential questions recently, particularly how one can live as a pious *and* prosperous Muslim in the globalised world. Born into a poor Muslim peasant family in 1986, Yang started working on the farm at the age of 15. He then migrated to other parts in the Northwest as a construction worker. Yang's paternal grandfather, who used to be a respected trader and was attacked as a 'capitalist profiteer' during the Cultural Revolution, urged Yang to attend a madrasa – an informal Islamic school – that was part of the local mosque, to find the right path in his life. Yang learned the basic alphabet, but he quit after three months because life in the madrasa was just too boring.

Yang then enrolled in an Arabic language school in a neighbouring province. Having emerged the end of the 1970s, Arabic language schools are small private colleges set up by Muslim charities to teach Islam through modern Arabic, rather than through a mixture of ancient Arabic, Persian and Chinese as madrasas in China do. Most of the students were Muslim youths who had dropped out of state middle schools as they did not feel that they would benefit from formal education. Aimed at providing alternative educational opportunities to these Muslim youths, the Arabic language schools model themselves after mainstream vocational colleges. They have classrooms and use blackboards, which Yang preferred to sitting on the floor memorising scripts as madrasa students do. He was also pleased that students in Arabic language schools could ask challenging questions. This made him ponder deeper questions.

On graduation, Yang planned to go overseas, but he could not get a passport. He worked as an assistant imam in charge of the madrasa in a mosque, but he did not like it because 'you can't think deeply in a mosque'. He came to Guangzhou in 2008 to become an interpreter, following successful examples among his friends. After one month's searching and waiting, Yang found his first job with a trading company owned by a Palestinian. The monthly salary was RMB1,500 (US$187), which was less than 40% of the average income in the city (RMB 3,780 in 2008). 'I took whatever he offered. My main purpose was to survive, to learn to listen and speak [Arabic]'. Yang accompanied the boss's clients on visits to wholesale markets and factories around Guangzhou, followed up with suppliers in China throughout the process of manufacturing, inspected goods before they were delivered to shipping agencies and, after that, helped to settle the payments. As Yang was the only employee in the company, he had to do everything. He worked 12 hours a day. His bedroom in the basement was so damp that, in the rainy season, he could squeeze water out of his quilt in the morning.

A year later, more confident in his Arabic, Yang moved to a larger company, run by an Egyptian trader, but soon jumped ship again to join a Yemeni company. His salary went up to RMB 5,000 a month. In addition, he received tips from some of the visiting clients, about US$100 for a week's tour. Chinese suppliers sometimes also paid interpreters commissions, normally 0.5–1% of the total amount, often given as 'tea money'. When an Egyptian client whom Yang had worked with before suggested that Yang could work for him as a buying agent to source goods in China, Yang agreed. Yang thus became self-employed. He also established stable work relations with two traders in Algeria. All the traders specialised in women's and children's clothes. The Egyptian and Algerian traders visited China once or twice a year to search for new products. Otherwise, they delegated all the tasks related to procurement and exports to Yang. Yang's annual exports value averaged RMB 6 million, from which he charged a commission ranging from 3.5% to 5%. The revenue after 2013, however, dropped to about RMB 2 million due to the global economic slowdown; the commission rate went down to as low as 2%.

With more free time on his hands now, Yang partied more (he and his family rented a two-bedroom apartment in a neighbourhood with more than 50 Hui families from the north-west; they hosted dinner parties for each other constantly), read more, in both Chinese and Arabic, and reflected on faith more deeply. A key question that Yang and his fellow interpreters debated concerned the relationship between Islam and China. Yang was rather critical of the popular suggestion that Muslims in China ought to 'de-Sinicise' themselves, for instance by abandoning Han rituals of life events, and 'return' to the Quranic roots. Yang suggested that this was simply impossible to do, as there are thousands of interpretation texts about the Quran, including dozens that are widely circulated in China: 'What are you returning to?' Furthermore, it does not make sense to talk about de-Sinicising Islam because the Han culture is already covered by Islam.

> Islam is universal and flexible; it does not target any particular people.... There are different interpretations because the environments are different. You can't drive polar bears to [tropical] Hainan Island.

Yang further emphasised the importance of scholars who bridge universalistic Islam and specific contexts of material life:

> Scholars are our medium to maintain and understand the essence of our religion. They are carriers of our tradition. Now, in the name of returning to the Quran, some people attack this or that scholar. They don't take into account at all the contexts of these scholars' writings at that time. If you don't understand the context, you will not get the essence of knowledge.

Yang's understanding of the importance of the medium makes him more accepting than others of government policies regarding religion. For instance, he stressed the merit of government-run

Islamic colleges to train officially recognised imams: 'The government colleges are a window of communication. The government needs to train people who understand religion as well as policy and law.' The biggest problem facing Islam in China today, Yang suggested, is not the lack of freedom, but the lack of a Chinese way to bridge global Islamic tradition with Chinese reality. In other words, what is needed is a right interpretation.

I lost contact with Yang and many of our common friends after 2017. The Chinese government tightened its control over religion in general, and Islam in particular. All the informal mosques set up by the interpreters in Guangzhou were shut down. Most books related to Islam were removed from bookshops. I had to put my project aside halfway through. I am confident that Yang and his fellow interpreters will survive and re-emerge one day, just as their ancestors have done for a long time. It is sad, however, that those in power lag behind Yang so much in appreciating the art of mediation and interpretation.

Yenny

by Jorge Alvis

Yenny is no longer just an interpreter of Colombian Sign Language (LSC). She was one, and she still occasionally performs as such, but currently she wears different hats as a professional. For one, she works as a linguist, which in Colombia means that you are a teacher. Until the spring semester of 2019, Yenny taught at three colleges in Bogotá. At other times, she is a researcher in the sociolinguistics of sign languages, and an advisor for both private and official institutions in topics like language, culture and education of deaf students.

There is an anecdote that highlights the sharp edges of her various roles around sign languages in Colombia. Once, at a national conference, Yenny was presenting, in oral Spanish, some results from a research project on the standardization of lexical signs in the semantic field of sports, when a deaf girl interrupted and questioned her in front of the audience, asking why she was talking about LSC if she was "just an interpreter." As a native oral speaker of Spanish, she didn't own the sign language.

Yenny was a well-known interpreter within the deaf community in Bogotá, first in the churches and later at schools. She had been a member of the Jehovah's Witnesses, whose churches and groups have served as a nest for the development of sign language in Colombian cities, while simultaneously creating the conditions for the emergence of a sense of language community enmeshed with religious beliefs. It was one of Yenny's brothers, like their parents a member of the church, who brought LSC into their home. And she was immediately captivated.

Yenny broke her ties with the church after experiencing the restrictions that community rules imposed on her interactions with her siblings and a beloved friend. It was a deep personal rupture, a time she doesn't like to talk about. She left the church, but never quit LSC.

Later, after passing a qualification exam, she was recruited by Fenascol (Federación Nacional de Sordos de Colombia, the National Federation of the Deaf in Colombia) to work as an interpreter at a high school in Bogotá. Her knowledge was basic, but good enough to be hired. Those were the times when the job market for LSC interpreters was booming in Bogotá, due to the implementation of an inclusion policy at schools. Deaf students joined regular classes with oral speakers of Spanish and they followed the same curriculum. From one day to the next, interpreters were mandatory. No one in the education system seemed to be completely ready for the task.

Back then, in her "golden age," Yenny's schedule on weekdays was as follows: She worked from 6am to noon at one school, then had lunch. Then, she worked occasionally from 2 to 4pm in activities for the social inclusion of deaf people. She had a break of around two hours again in the afternoon before working continuously from 6 to 10pm at night school. Roughly 40 hours a week of interpretation. As she worked from dawn till dusk with sign language, her competences improved. She became a fluent user and a seasoned interpreter with first-hand knowledge of the lives and struggles of deaf students. But she got ill too. She had to use a splint and regularly visit her physio-therapist due to long-standing tendonitis.

By the time her stance was publicly disputed in public by the deaf girl at the conference, Yenny had gained vast experience in the social and cultural issues around LSC. And she was also pursuing an academic path: Yenny had received her BA in linguistics at the Universidad Nacional de Colombia and her MA from the Instituto Caro y Cuervo, a center for language and literature research in Bogotá, where she graduated with honors with a dissertation on the sign language of Providence Island. Even though Yenny recounted the episode quite incidentally and off the record when I interviewed her, I found it to be a key moment in her professional life that serves as a window to current disputes around language, power struggles and deaf identity in Colombia.

I asked Yenny what she replied to the girl. She didn't recall the exact words or signs, but remembered saying in LSC that she played many roles in her life. She was not only a person paid by people and institutions to interpret, translate and mediate between the deaf and the hearing. She emphasized that being an interpreter was her job, but it didn't define her identity. She wasn't a one-sided, unidimensional subject; she was also a woman, a mother, and a linguist. And yes, definitely yes, she could lecture on the LSC standardization process, because she had formally investigated it.

The tensions around the identities mobilized by the use of LSC are so vivid that, in one of her recent reflexive pieces (still in press) written as a contribution to a book that will commemorate the first 20 years of the linguistics major at the Universidad Nacional de Colombia, Yenny reveals that being an interpreter became the main obstacle to her work as a linguist. She found herself trapped in the long-standing discussion around the essentialist native/non-native duality and had to fight back to move on as a researcher.

There are two lively fields of struggle that converge in Yenny's professional life. Actually, they go beyond her particular case and have run through the related linguistic, political and institutional fields since the mid-1990s. The first is related to repeated but unsuccessful attempts to devise an accreditation protocol or certificate for sign language interpretation as a professional trade. The second is the internal schism in the national deaf community around the lexical innovations proposed by a group called Árbol de Vida (Tree of Life). I dare say that Yenny, due to her track record, has been a witness of privilege and an increasingly empowered protagonist in these two fields.

Regarding the first field, no formal certificate or degree is needed to exercise the position of an LSC interpreter in Colombia. Interpretation consists mostly in translating oral Spanish into LSC for the deaf community. As it is, almost every state-sponsored television broadcast in Colombia includes LSC interpretation, but not all interpreters on the screen are professionals – a situation that is reminiscent of the "fake interpreter" in South Africa at Nelson Mandela's memorial ceremony in 2013. Standing next to President Barack Obama, the fake interpreter was just "literally flapping his arms around" (Euronews, 11 December 2013).

For Yenny, having a certificate might help improve the quality of interpretation and would benefit everybody: interpreters themselves, employers and deaf people. It would work as a formal qualification of the knowledge of the language and the basic principles of interpretation. To date, according to her, you can go to any remote village in Colombia and tell the mayor that she/he is legally obliged to hire you, but no one in the administration will know if you have proper training as an interpreter.

The fact is that many interpreters have only a basic knowledge of the language and a lot of (unassessed) practice. This is not the case for Yenny, however, who has moved steadily from practice towards formal training and research, from a subordinate position in the job market to a better one where she feels she can decide who her clients and employers will be. Since her early years of practice, Yenny has been a member of several organizations of interpreters, most of them currently inactive. As mentioned, she has worked for Fenascol, the strongest organization of deaf people in Colombia, where she oversaw an agreement to provide LSC interpreters to public schools in Bogotá. She also held a position at the Insor (the National Institute of the Deaf), which is the public language policy-maker. Moreover, she graduated from two of the most prestigious centers in the country. Finally, she has published in national and international journals on the linguistics of sign languages. In sum, she has built a solid profile and gained a prominent position, allowing her to stand out among her former colleagues nationwide – if not yet in salary, at least symbolically.

Pay rates have stagnated since the beginning of the 2000s. The range is very broad, and conditions for signing a contract are not stable. For instance, if an interpreter is hired directly, wages are between US$8 and US$17 per hour of interpretation, depending on the client. If it's outsourced, i.e. someone like Fenascol mediates the deal, the interpreter only receives between US$7 and US$9 per hour. Yenny's main income nowadays comes from teaching as an adjunct, although she hasn't quit interpretation. Indeed, she is active as a freelancer and struggles to avoid people who take advantage of her expertise and knowledge. She has fresh memories of a disingenuous negotiation where she was invited to submit her résumé to a company, with the promise that they would hire her because of her outstanding profile. But they never called her back. Afterwards, she was told by a trusted colleague that the company had presented her as one of the experts on their payroll to win new business with public funds. The case illustrates that people, institutions and companies can play dirty to benefit from skilled professionals in a job market where no accreditation is mandatory.

The second field of tension that crisscrosses Yenny's professional life is the aforementioned division around lexical innovations proposed by a "belligerent" group of the deaf, as they were portrayed in a recent paper by two linguistic anthropologists. Árbol de Vida (AdV) was initially a group of deaf high school students who took the initiative, in the mid-1990s, of creating new signs to fulfill their need for academic vocabulary and concepts in LSC. Ever since, their neologisms have been rejected by older community leaders as an "unnatural" development of the language, or an "impure" interference in the beauty and expressiveness of LSC. In spite of this criticism, they haven't ceased their work of "upgrading" the language to make it fit new and challenging social contexts. With time, the conflict has escalated to new levels, deepening the schism: the use of AdV signs has been banned in public schools at the suggestion of Fenascol.

In Yenny's eyes, the internal clash is paradoxical and disquieting, to say the least. Not so many years ago, deaf people were oppressed by the hearing majority in schools and churches. History repeats itself with irony: nowadays, those who condemn the use of a variety of LSC are the same people whose language was silenced in the past. "Actually, the problem is about politics, not language," Yenny concludes. Her personal choice has been to act politically too, by supporting the AdV cause. Last semester, Yenny became an advisor to Josue, the AdV's leader, who is pursuing, as she did, a master's in linguistics, and is also working with his comrades to open new paths for the understanding of the deaf world in Colombia.

Reference

Euronews (2013) Mandela Memorial Sign Language Interpreter a 'Fraud'. Available at https://www.euronews.com/2013/12/11/mandela-memorial-sign-language-interpreter-a-fraud.